THE RIMERS OF ELDRITCH
and Other Plays

ALSO BY LANFORD WILSON:

Balm in Gilead and Other Plays

The Rimers of Eldritch

AND OTHER PLAYS

by

LANFORD WILSON

A MERMAID DRAMABOOK

HILL AND WANG · NEW YORK

A DIVISION OF FARRAR, STRAUS AND GIROUX

For Joseph Cino

CONTENTS

THE RIMERS OF ELDRITCH

A *Play in Two Acts*

*The harvest is past, the summer is ended, and
we are not saved.*—Jer. 8:20

The Rimers of Eldritch was first presented by Ellen Stewart at La MaMa Experimental Theater Club, New York City on July 13, 1966 with the following cast:

ROBERT CONKLIN	Michael Warren Powell
EVA JACKSON	Claris Erickson
EVELYN JACKSON	Tanya Berezin
NELLY WINDROD	Blanche Dee
MARY WINDROD	Shellie Feldman
PATSY JOHNSON	Beth Porter
MAVIS JOHNSON	Kay C. Coulthard
PECK JOHNSON	Gene Alton
JOSH JOHNSON	Marvin Alexander
LENA TRUIT	Jane Buchanan
MARTHA TRUIT	Ann Harris
WILMA ATKINS	Jacque Lynn Colton
SKELLY MANNOR	Robert Thirkield
PREACHER/JUDGE	George Harris
CORA GROVES	Kay Carney
WALTER	Fred Forrest
TRUCKER	Oliver Dixon

The play was directed by the author; the stage manager was Lola Richardson.

The play was subsequently presented at the Cherry Lane Theater in New York by Theater 1967, directed by Michael Kahn and designed by William Ritman.

CHARACTERS

ROBERT CONKLIN, *a boy, eighteen*
EVA JACKSON, *a crippled girl, fourteen*
EVELYN JACKSON, *her mother*
NELLY WINDROD, *a strong woman, middle-aged*
MARY WINDROD, *her senile mother*
PATSY JOHNSON, *the prettiest girl at Centerville High*
MAVIS JOHNSON, *her mother*
PECK JOHNSON, *her father*
JOSH JOHNSON, *her brother*
LENA TRUIT, *her girl friend, the same age*
MARTHA TRUIT, *Lena's mother*
WILMA ATKINS, *a friend of Martha's*
SKELLY MANNOR, *the town hermit, about sixty*
PREACHER ⎫
JUDGE ⎭ *played by the same actor, in mid-fifties*
CORA GROVES, *the owner of Hilltop Café*
WALTER, *her lover*
A TRUCKER

The locale of the play is Eldritch, present population about seventy, one of the many nearly abandoned towns in America's Middle West. The time is the present.

The play takes place during the spring, summer, and fall of the year, skipping at will from summer back to spring or forward to fall and from one conversation to another. All the characters are on stage throughout the play, except twice as indicated, grouping as needed to suggest time and place.

At La MaMa Experimental Theater Club and the Cherry Lane Theater the play was acted on a series of six or eight descending, irregular levels, some with railings to suggest a porch or the witness stand of the courtroom as needed, against a black void. It might also be done with various architectural elements, suggested gables, trees, ruined buildings, American Gothic motifs indicating the various buildings of the town.

The lighting, especially if a bare stage or platforms are used, might be considered the most important single scenic element. In this edition—to assist the readers in *seeing* the play—it has been indicated at the beginning of each scene where the conversations take place. Some are quite obvious: scenes in the café, court, or church. Others, such as "A *street in town*," a director might wish to place elsewhere; they should be thought of only as suggestions to aid in following the printed text of the play. A scene continues—sometimes two or more in separate areas of the stage simultaneously—until the lights dim on the scene and focus attention elsewhere.

THE RIMERS OF ELDRITCH

ACT ONE

In darkness, WILMA *and* MARTHA *on the porch of* MARTHA'S *house.*

WILMA. Well, what I heard isn't fit for talk, but I heard that Mrs. Cora Groves, up on the highway . . . ?

MARTHA. Yes.

WILMA. . . . has taken a boy, she's old enough to be his mother on, and is keeping him up there in her café.

MARTHA. In her bed.

WILMA [*with true sympathy*]. That woman went crazy when her husband left her.

MARTHA. Oh, I know she did.

WILMA. That woman, I swear, isn't responsible for her own actions.

A very faint light begins to illuminate the courtroom, NELLY *standing, her hand raised.*

MARTHA. I should say she isn't.

WILMA. I hear he does things around the café, whistling around like he belonged there.

MARTHA. Have you ever heard anything like it?

WILMA. I haven't, I swear to God.

A sharp increase in the lights.

In the courtroom.

NELLY. I do.

MARTHA'S porch—morning.

MARTHA. Why, she called Evelyn Jackson a liar to her face, and Eva too. Swore things the devil and his angels wouldn't believe it. She'd stand up there and swear black was white.

WILMA. And Nelly, poor woman, the life that woman leads. Only God in His Heaven knows the trials that woman has to bear.

MARTHA. That she should have to be dragged through this.

WILMA. She stood there and told the way it was; I said to Mrs. Jackson—cried the whole time——

MARTHA. —I know, I saw.

5

WILMA. —Only God in Heaven knows the trials that poor woman has had to bear.

In the courtroom.

JUDGE. Nelly Windrod, do you solemnly swear to tell the whole truth, and nothing but the truth——

NELLY [*quietly troubled*]. I do, yes.

JUDGE. —so help you God?

NELLY. I do.

JUDGE [*exactly as before*]. Nelly Windrod, do you solemnly swear to tell the whole truth, and nothing but the truth——

NELLY. I do, yes.

JUDGE. —so help you God?

NELLY. I do.

MARTHA's porch—night.

MARTHA. So help me God I don't know how we let him hang around here like he did. Not talking to nobody.

WILMA. Nobody I know of could live like that.

MARTHA. Like that time he scared young Patsy so bad.

WILMA. Bad for the whole town with someone like that.

MARTHA. Like that way he had of just standing around.

WILMA. Around here everybody knows everybody.

MARTHA. Everybody was scared of him. Everybody knew what he was.

WILMA. A fool like that.

MARTHA. Grumbling and mumbling around; standing and watching it all.

WILMA. I'd think people'd feel easier now. I know I swear I do.

MARTHA. I do.

In the courtroom.

NELLY. I do.

Beat.

JUDGE [*faintly, fading*]. Now, Miss Windrod, if you would tell the court, in your own words . . .

In the grocery where ROBERT works.

MARY [*to* ROBERT]. Now, we have to understand that Nelly is my flesh and blood.

ROBERT. I know.

MARY. Yes, love, she's my flesh and blood and she thinks she knows but she doesn't know but she thinks she does.

ROBERT. I suppose she does if anybody does.

MARY. Well, she thinks she does. But I know and you know. I was at my window, watching the moon.

ROBERT. Was there a moon?

MARY. I said to those people, all those new people in town—there isn't much to know about Eldritch, used to be Elvin Eldritch's pasture till it gave out I guess and they found coal. It was built on coal with coal money and deserted when the coal gave out and here it stands, this wicked old town. All the buildings bowing and nodding.

ROBERT. How do you know so much?

MARY. And still so little? I would puzzle that if I could. I told them none of the people here now were coal people. The mining people moved off; they raped the land and moved away. There used to be explosives that rattled the windows, oh my, and shook the water in a bucket, day and night.

ROBERT. How come you remember so much?

MARY. And still so little? The last time I saw you, why, you was just a little baby; you've grown up so.

ROBERT. You saw me yesterday, Mrs. Windrod.

MARY. You don't know. Isn't that sweet. The last time I saw you, why, you weren't no bigger than that high.

ROBERT. You've known me all my——

MARY. You've grown up so. I have terrible bruises on my arm there. Look at that.

CORA's *café*. WALTER *is sitting at the counter.*

TRUCKER [*leaving*]. I'll see you, Cora.

CORA. Can't avoid it, I guess. You watch it now on those narrow roads.

TRUCKER. It's push-pull with the load; I'll come back through empty day after tomorrow—you remember to tell me that again.

CORA. Stay awake now.

TRUCKER. No danger of that.

On the porch.

WILMA. I'll say one thing for her. How long has it been he's been there?

CORA [*to* WALTER]. Boy.

MARTHA. Two or three months now nearly. Walks around the place whistling like he owned it.

WILMA. Well, he earns his keep.

CORA. Boy.

MARTHA. It's not in the kitchen that he earns his keep, Wilma.

CORA. Boy.

WILMA. Well, I'll say one thing——

CORA. —I'm getting ready to close up now.

WILMA.—Whatever it is, she looks a darn sight better now than she did a year ago. Since I can remember.

CORA. Boy.

WALTER [*as though waking from a daydream*]. I'm sorry.

CORA. I'm fixing to close up. You sleeping?

WALTER. Thinking, I guess.

CORA. Have another cup of coffee, I got time.

MARTHA. That woman isn't responsible for her own actions since her husband left her.

WALTER. Swell.

WILMA. It's not for us to judge.

MARTHA. That's all well and good but anyone who deliberately cuts herself off from everybody else in town.

WILMA. I don't judge, but I know who I speak to on the street and who I don't.

WALTER. Is there work here in town do you know?

CORA. Down in Eldritch? Not if you're looking for wages. Not here.

MARTHA. It's easy to see the devil's work.

WALTER. I had that in mind.

CORA. You might try Centerville; Eldritch is all but a ghost town.

WALTER. You here alone?

CORA. I've managed for seven years; it hasn't bothered me.

WALTER. It might not be a bad idea to take someone on yourself.

WILMA. It's a sin to sashay through Centerville the way she does, buying that boy shirts and new clothes. Keeping him up on the highway.

MARTHA. I don't go, but I understand he's made a show place out of her café.

WILMA. I'd be happier if it was me if they made her close it down.

MARTHA. It ought to be against the law serving beer to truck drivers and them having to be on the road so much.

WILMA. The wages of sin lead to death.

CORA. Aren't you cold in just that jacket; that's pretty light for April.

WALTER. No, it's not bad.

They regard each other a moment; the light fades on the café.

MARTHA. The wages of sin is death.

WILMA. Bless her heart, poor old thing.

MARTHA [*as* MARY WINDROD *passes the porch*]. Good evening, Mary.

WILMA. Good evening, Mary Windrod.

MARY [*stopping*]. You two. I watch you two sometimes.

MARY *talks, almost with everything she says, as though she were describing a beautiful dream to a pet canary.*

WILMA. Aren't you cold in that shawl, dear?

MARTHA. Nights are cold in this valley for June.

MARY. It's not bad.

WILMA. You'll be catching a chill next.

MARY. I was once a nurse and I believe that the constant proximity to sickness has given me an immunity to night air.

MARTHA. Never think that.

MARY. Us dry old women rattle like paper; we couldn't get sick. I listen to you old women sometimes.

WILMA. How's your daughter?

MARY. Yes, indeed.

MARTHA. I beg your pardon?

MARY. The proximity to all that sickness.

WILMA. Yes, love.

MARY. Immunity to death myself. My number passed Gabriel right on by. It came up and passed right on by and here I am a forgotten child.

WILMA. You better get inside, love.

MARY. Rusting away, flaking away.

MARTHA. You get in, now.

MARY [leaving]. This wicked town. God hear a dried-up woman's prayer and do not forgive this wicked town!

The CONGREGATION bursts into "Shall We Gather at the River"; after only a few bars, the song stops abruptly.

In the courtroom.

NELLY. And Mama came running downstairs and said a man had attacked young Eva Jackson.

JUDGE. Would you point out Eva . . . ?

NELLY [as the light fades]. There, poor lamb, can't hardly speak two words since this thing happened and I don't wonder——

On the porch.

WILMA [overlapping a word or two]. Well, I know I swear I don't know what he sees in her.

MARTHA. It's nice of him, though.

WILMA. Well, I know but Driver Junior's old enough to be taking girls out; he shouldn't be wandering around with her.

MARTHA. It's nice to have somebody to keep her company. Still and all, it doesn't seem natural, I know what you mean.

WILMA. I don't know what he sees in her.

MARTHA. Poor thing.

Near EVA's house.

ROBERT. Eva!

EVA. Are you glad to be out of school?

ROBERT. I liked it all right.

EVA. What are you going to be?

ROBERT. Who knows?

EVA. We had our Eighth Grade graduation in robes! I bet I know what you won't be, don't I?

ROBERT. What's that?

EVA. A race car driver.

ROBERT. Why do you want to say that? You think I couldn't do that if I wanted to?

EVA. You don't want to get yourself killed.

ROBERT. Driver didn't want it; he just had an accident.

EVA. You want to be like him?

ROBERT. People don't want to do the same thing their brother did; I couldn't see any sense in it.

EVA. I knew you didn't. You aren't going to get yourself killed.

ROBERT. Killed doesn't have anything to do with it. Eva, good Lord, I don't want people carrying on like that; honking their horns, coming into town every week like a parade. I never even went to see Driver.

EVA. You decided what you want to be?

ROBERT. I don't have to decide this minute, do I?

EVA. I just wondered.

ROBERT. Do you know? You don't know what you want.

EVA. Of course I know; you know, I told you. So do you know, everybody knows what they want—it's what they think they really can do that they don't know.

ROBERT. Well, I don't have to decide yet.

EVA [*in a sudden burst, as though conjuring*]. When's it gonna be autumn? I love autumn so much I could hug it. I want it to be autumn. That's what I want right now. Now! Autumn! Now!

ROBERT. Good luck; I don't see it.

EVA [*in a burst*]. Don't you be derisive to me, Driver Junior!

ROBERT. Don't call me that.

EVA. Well, don't you go on, Robert Conklin, or I'll call you anything I like.

ROBERT. You'll be talking to yourself.

EVA. Everybody else calls you that. Don't go away; I won't, I promise. Don't you wish it was autumn? Don't you? Don't you love autumn? And the wind and rime and pumpkins and gourds and corn shocks? I won't again. Don't you love autumn? Don't you, Robert? I won't call you that. Everybody else does but I won't.

ROBERT. I haven't thought about it.

EVA. Well, think about it, right now. Think about how it smells.

ROBERT. How does it smell?

EVA. Like dry, windy, cold, frosty rime and chaff and leaf smoke and corn husks.

ROBERT. It does, huh?

EVA. Pretend. Close your eyes—are your eyes closed? Don't you wish it was here? Like apples and cider. *You* go.

ROBERT. And rain.

EVA. Sometimes. And potatoes and flower seeds and honey.

ROBERT. And popcorn and butter.

EVA [*opening her eyes*]. Yes. Oh, it does not! You're not playing at all. There's hay and clover and alfalfa and all that. [*Hitting him, really quite hard, slapping.*]

ROBERT [*laughing*]. Come on, it's different for everybody.

EVA. Well, that's not right; it doesn't at all. Are you making fun?

ROBERT. Come on, don't be rough.

EVA. I will too; you're not the least bit funny, Driver Junior! [*As he starts to walk on.*] Come back here, Robert! Robert Conklin. Driver Junior! Little brother. Your brother was a man, anyway. Coward. Robert? Bobby?

In the store.

WILMA. And I'll have some flour and yeast. And three packs of Sure-jell.

ROBERT. Right you are. How much flour?

WILMA. No more than five pounds in this weather. How're you doing in school?

ROBERT. All right.

WILMA. I just said to Martha Truit, I suppose Driver Junior will be leaving us as soon as school gets out next month, like all the young kids now.

ROBERT. Not for a while yet.

WILMA. Oh, you will; you'll be going off to see the world.

ROBERT. I don't know.

WILMA. There's nothing for a strong young man in this dead old town. Where do you think you'll be heading?

ROBERT. I don't know.

WILMA. Des Moines?

ROBERT. I don't imagine.

WILMA. St. Louis?

ROBERT. Who knows?

WILMA. Chicago?

ROBERT. I might not leave at all for a while.

WILMA. Well, your brother stayed and he was wonderful, but we all expect you to be moving along like all the young boys now.

ROBERT. I don't know.

Downstairs in the Windrod house. NELLY has a hold on MARY's arm. MARY is turning backward, NELLY forward, MARY avoiding the raised hand threatening her, much as on a turntable going backward.

MARY. I know, I know, I know, I know, don't hit me; don't hit me, baby.

NELLY. What do you mean telling people a tale like that. You know I bought that mill.

MARY. You bought it, baby; I know you bought it.

NELLY. Well, they said in town you told I'd killed Dad to get it.

MARY. I said he died mysteriously.

NELLY. Well, he died of old age; he was ninety-six, for God's sakes.

MARY. He died mysteriously!

NELLY. In his sleep like you will; died of old age like you will. What in hell do you mean telling something like that?

MARY. I didn't mean to, baby. I don't mean to——

NELLY. —You're batty as a goddamned loon.

MARY. They don't like me is what it is. They know I watch them. They don't like me in town, I knew they didn't. I don't say those things. They tell things on me.

NELLY. You're crazy as hell is what it is; you're out of your god-damned mind is what it is.

MARY. Baby, don't talk like that. They tell *fibs* on me. They say——

NELLY. Showing them bruises and saying I beat you; when the hell did I ever beat you? You know goddamned well how you get those bruises. You fall down! You bruise! You run into things! You're old. You bump things. Who the hell takes care of you and you telling lies on me like that, Mama—what do you mean?

MARY. I don't mean to.

NELLY. They don't listen to you—to say things like that.

MARY. They don't listen to me, Nelly.

NELLY. It doesn't do you any good; they come right in and tell me.

MARY. Don't hurt me.

NELLY. I think you better go on up to your room!

MARY. No, don't lock the door.

NELLY. If I leave the house, I'll lock the door or you'll wander out and get hurt. You'll fall down the stairs and tell I beat you.

MARY. I don't want to go up there; the evil town is all around me up there.

NELLY. Go upstairs, Mama.

MARY. It's painted on the windows——

NELLY. Well, pull the shades down if you don't want to see them. [*She leaves.*]

MARY. My skin, whole body is just flaking away—this evil town! This evil town!

On a street in town: JOSH *and all the young men in the cast except* WALTER.

BOYS [*taunting* SKELLY, *jeeringly*]. Baaaaaaaaaaa! Baaaaaaaaaa! Baaaaaaaaaa! Baaaaaaaaa!

SKELLY [*in a deep, mangled, growling, almost drunken voice*]. Get on, you son of bitch. Son of bitches. [*Sounding about like "Geah-own-ya-sansobith! Sansobith!"*]

BOYS. Baaaaaa! Baaaaaa!

SKELLY. Get the hell on, you, get on! [*In a deep, almost terrified growl.*] Go, go on, sonabith!

In the courtroom.

NELLY. And I heard something outside——

The town becomes alive everywhere. PECK, NELLY, MARY, JOSH, MARTHA *and the* JUDGE *are in the court,* PATSY *and* LENA *in town;*

EVELYN *is walking out onto her porch calling* EVA, *who is approaching the porch. An area may be* EVELYN's *porch and part of the courtroom at the same time—the effect should be of the entire cast moving in a deliberate direction with lines coming in sequence from all over the stage.* CORA *enters the café area from upstairs, sleepily, calling softly, exactly as she will when the scene is repeated at the end of the first act.*

JUDGE. A travesty of justice.

PECK. We, the jury——

CORA. Walter?

PECK. —find Nelly Windrod——

CORA. Walter?

PECK. —not guilty.

MARTHA. Not guilty.

CORA. Walter?

EVA. Robert?

NELLY. Oh, God; Mama?

EVELYN. Eva?

TRUCKER. Not guilty.

WILMA. Papa?

MAVIS. Peck?

JOSH. Not guilty. [*He begins whistling softly, calling a dog.*] Here, Blackie, here, boy.

WALTER. Cora!

CORA. Walter?

JUDGE. Not guilty.

PATSY. I know.

EVELYN. Eva? You come on, now.

CORA. Oh, God, oh, God, oh, God, oh, God, oh, God.

JOSH. Blackie? Here, Blackie?

EVELYN. You better get on in here now.

EVA. I'm coming.

JOSH. Come on, boy.

LENA. The poor thing.

PATSY. Really, I get so damn tired of all that nonsense.

LENA. I know, but they insist I wear it.

The movement subsides.

EVELYN [*continuing*]. You better put a sweater on if you're going to sit out there.

EVA [*approaching the house*]. I'm coming in directly.

EVELYN. Not directly, you come on in now.

EVA. All right.

EVELYN. Where were you all day?

EVA. I was wandering around the woods.

EVELYN. Now, you know I don't want you running around alone. What if you fell and hurt yourself and who'd ever know it?

EVA. I wasn't alone; Robert and I went walking.

EVELYN. Well, don't you go off alone.

EVA. I won't.

EVELYN. Not all afternoon. Wandering around; God knows what could happen to you.

EVA. I know, I don't.

EVELYN. You look so fatigued.

EVA. I'm not at all.

EVELYN. I don't want you spending so much time with that boy.

EVA. What boy?

EVELYN. That Driver Junior. Wandering around with that boy. Spending all afternoon and evening with him.

EVA. Well, who else would I spend it with?

EVELYN. Well, why do you have to go off every day of the week? Doing God knows what? You could visit the Stutses, you shouldn't be running around. It isn't good for you; you have to be careful. You're not like other kids; you know how easily you get fatigued; you run yourself out every day; perspiring like you do; wandering off with that boy. If something happened, who'd know? And don't think he's responsible; his brother might have been different; devil and his angels wouldn't know if something happened. I don't know why you can't stay at home like everyone else. Traipsing around the woods half-naked, what do you do out there in the woods alone, the two of you, anyhow?

EVA. Nothing.

EVELYN. I said you answer me.

EVA [*rapidly*]. Nothing!

EVELYN. I said you answer me the truth, young miss.

EVA. We don't do anything. Whatever you think.

EVELYN. Don't you talk back to me, what do you do, little miss smarty pants? All day gone from the house, smarty? [*Hits her.*]

EVA. We talk.

EVELYN. You talk, you talk, I'll just bet you talk; now you get in that house this minute do you hear me!

EVA [*running to the witness stand*]. I don't know what you think.

EVELYN. You get on in to the supper table! You're going to be the death of me. I swear, I swear, I swear.

Everyone is assembled in court.

JUDGE. —to tell the whole truth and nothing but the truth, so help you God?

ROBERT. She didn't see anything.

JUDGE. Eva, as a witness to this terrible——

EVA. I don't know! I didn't see! I didn't see! I told you I didn't see anything! [*A long run into her* MOTHER's *open arms.*]

EVA. Mama.

EVELYN. Leave my daughter alone! Can't you see she's upset? My God, what are you trying to do to her?

CORA. She told me.

EVELYN [*to* EVA]. Poor baby—— [*To* CORA.] You know what I think of you? Before God!

CORA. I talked to her; she told me.

ROBERT [*his lines overlapping* CORA's]. She didn't see.

EVA. I don't know!

NELLY. It's not true, none of it, it's like I said. You're trying to make a murderer of me; it was God's will be done.

JUDGE [*his voice rising above theirs, simultaneously, trying to quiet them*]. We have all long known Skelly Mannor; we have known of his past— that latent evil in him, that unnatural desire, and we have long been aware that at any time the bitterness in his soul might again overflow. [*Gen-*

CORA. She told me!

eral crowd murmur.] We let things lie. We took no action to prevent his crime—the pending, at any moment, crime—we all knew it—and the burden must be ours. We are responsible for the shock to these two innocents.

The others have been quieted. General murmur in response to the JUDGE. *Several Amens.*

JUDGE [*continuing*]. We are responsible for our actions; for allowing the heathen in our fold!

The JUDGE's *oratory slides into the* PREACHER. *We are at church.*

CONGREGATION. Amen!

PREACHER. God forgive us.

CONGREGATION. Amen.

PREACHER. In Your wisdom forgive us. And help these two souls, these two innocent souls forget that dark moment.

CONGREGATION. Amen, amen.

PREACHER. Blind them to that dark moment and set them free, Lord.

CONGREGATION. Amen.

PREACHER. Dear Lord.

CONGREGATION. Amen.

PREACHER. Our Saviour!

In the café.

WALTER [*to* CORA]. Where do you want the pie?

CORA [*warmly, chiding*]. On the rack that says "pies."

WALTER. And the coffee in the jar that says "coffee" and the typed-up menus in the menu covers? I'll catch on.

CORA. You're doing fine.

WALTER. Well, for only a week.

CORA. You'll catch on.

In the congregation MARTHA *says, very faintly,* "A show place," *echoed by* "I hear" *from* WILMA.

WALTER [*overlapping*]. And you have to consider that we spend more time upstairs than down, or I'd know a lot more about the restaurant business and a lot less about you.

CORA. Now you just clam up before somebody comes in.

WALTER. Ashamed, are you?

CORA. No, I most certainly am not and you know it, but I don't intend to bother someone else's business with my own.

WALTER. Wonder what they think?

CORA. You do, do you?

WALTER. "No, I most certainly do not and you know it"—I like the way you people talk. You're looking good.

CORA. I'm feeling good.

WALTER. What would you think about putting an awning over the door so a fellow doesn't get soaking wet with rain as soon as he steps out the door.

CORA. Hm. What'd I care if he's going out?

WALTER. Oh, it might be that on the way out is when he decides to come back.

CORA. You think, do you?

WALTER. "You think, do you?" It's something to consider.

WILMA. A show place.

The Johnson house.

PATSY. It's a trash heap is what it is. I don't know what keeps us here; I swear I don't. Maybe it was all right when you were young. The only people who ever comes into town is people to drive around looking around, poking around to see what a ghost town looks like. Movie house been closed down eight years; you want to see a movie you have to drive twenty miles into Centerville. Every building on Main Street closed up, falling down except a store and a grubby filling station. Boys stand out, hanging around, it's a disgrace——

On her porch.

EVELYN. —Can't be healthy, rats took over the old grainery, all the buildings rotting and falling down, the mine shaft building used to just shine; you could see it miles away; now the way it sags— falling apart, boarded together; everything flapping and rusting, it's an absolute eyesore. Cats poking around through the rotting ruins of all those old buildings, their bellies just busting, it can't be healthy——

PATSY. —Dad could get a job in Centerville as well as here; I don't know why we stay here, there's a lot of decent people there, they know how to have fun, but no. We have to stay here. The boys from Centerville *all* have cars, I'm so ashamed getting off that ugly smelly school bus with all those younger kids, squealing; I swear sometimes I think I'm just going to sit there and not budge all day. Just let them drive right into the parking lot and sit there in the hot sun all day broiling rather than get off that bus with the boys all standing around the front of the school watching. I just wish you knew—they're probably surprised I don't smell of cow manure.

PECK. Patsy.

PATSY. Well, I'm sorry but it's true. I wish you could see the way they dress! In the summertime the boys from Centerville drive by on the highway alongside the field and I'm up on the hay wagon like some common hired hand and they yell and honk and carry on so damn smart I just wish I could die.

MAVIS. Patsy June.

PATSY. Well, I'm sorry but I do. At night sometimes I just cry my eyes out. Night after night. I just cry myself to sleep; I hope you're satisfied——

EVELYN. —Trying to scratch a living together. Trying to keep strong——

PATSY [*leaving house; to* LENA]. —I'm sorry, but I do——

EVELYN. —Sometimes I don't even know why we try——

LENA [*on her porch*]. I said it's warm, for crying out loud; it's May; school's nearly out; I don't know why I have to wear that ugly old thing, you have the nicest clothes. I never have a danged thing.

PATSY. Well, all the boys were wearing cashmere sweaters with V necks and I said if they can have them I sure as hell can; the girls in my class just turned pea-green-purple. I said, well, they didn't have what I wanted in Centerville, this two-bit town, so I went along with Dad to Des Moines; you should have seen them.

LENA. Peggy was furious.

PATSY. Oh, she thinks she's so rich; she has absolutely no taste at all.

LENA. I know.

PATSY. Black and brown and blue and green; I said the other day, "Why, Peggy, you look exactly the color of Chuck Melton's two-toned Mercury." You should have seen her face.

LENA. I wish I could have.

PATSY [*as they walk away from the porch*]. Well, listen; Chuck thinks he's so damn smart himself. Yelling to me, you should hear the things they say. It'd make your ears burn. I told him and he should know, if he wants to come by and come up to the door and knock like some kind of respectable person, then I'd go out; but I'm not going to just fly out of the house like that. He thinks he's so damn smart, I don't care how long he sits out in front of the house in his damn car. Honking. He can honk all night for all I care.

MARTHA [*coming to the porch*]. Evelyn said a regular show place.

WILMA. I heard she closes up at ten every night now.

MARTHA. Oh, my . . .

WILMA [*leaving porch*]. Ours is not to judge.

MARTHA. Still I know what I know.

LENA [*joins her mother*]. I know he did it. Why would anyone want to poison a helpless dog?

MARTHA. He just looked up at me like he knew I'd help him and there wasn't anything I could do this time and I think he knew.

LENA. I don't understand somebody doing something like that.

MARTHA. There wasn't anything I could do. Just nothing at all.

LENA. Why?

MARTHA. I don't know, love.

LENA [*repeating, with same inflection*]. Why?

MARTHA. I don't know, love.

LENA. Why?

MARTHA. I don't know, love.

LENA. Just a helpless little dog, he was too old to hurt anybody. There's somebody poisoning dogs around here and that's the lowest, meanest thing in the world.

MARTHA. No one should cause an animal to suffer like that.

LENA. I know he did it, too. I know it was him.

MARTHA. Well, we can think what we think, but we can't do anything.

LENA. I've seen how they bark at him; you know that. A dog can tell an evil person; a dog can tell; they're all scared of him.

WILMA [coming to the porch]. Wickedest man; creeping through town, looking into things.

MARTHA. Peeping into girls' bedrooms; standing around looking like that.

WILMA. Who knows what's in someone's mind like that?

PATSY screams very loudly, running from her bedroom into the living room.

PECK [startled]. What in God's name?

PATSY. Oh, God, oh, God, oh, God, oh, God. In there.

MAVIS. What's wrong, baby?

PATSY. I saw him. I saw him. Oh, God, he was looking in the window. His face——

PECK. Who was? Answer me.

MAVIS. Skelly?

PATSY. Skelly. Skelly. Skelly was. Oh, God, you should have seen his eyes! And I was only in my pants. You should have seen him.

JOSH. I don't know what he could have seen.

MAVIS. That's enough out of you now.

PECK. Where was he?

PATSY. At my bedroom window, where do you think?

MAVIS. You're imagining things; you're dreaming.

PATSY. I wasn't asleep, I tell you; I just was getting ready for bed.

PECK. It's okay now, I'll go out.

PATSY. No, he's gone now, my God, I screamed and he ran away.

PECK [with some humor]. Well, I'd think he would.

JOSH. Wake the dead; what's he gonna see?

MAVIS. Don't you start.

PATSY [contrite]. I'm sorry.

MAVIS. For what?

JOSH. Sorry he didn't come on in probably.

PATSY. For scaring you so.

MAVIS. It's all right. My word, something like that, I'd think you would.

PATSY. Only I was just so scared.

MAVIS. Of course you would. [JOSH *is stifling a laugh*.] That's enough, Dad said.

PATSY. It was horrible.

MAVIS. It's all right now.

PATSY. I don't think I can go back in my room.

JOSH. Oh, good Lord.

PECK. Young man.

MAVIS. It's all right now.

PATSY. Can't I sleep with you tonight?

MAVIS. It's all right now.

PATSY. Just tonight.

MAVIS. No, now, he's gone.

JOSH. What are you, some kind of baby?

PATSY. I was just so scared.

MAVIS. Go on back to bed, honey.

PATSY. I'm sorry.

MAVIS. It's okay.

PATSY. It was horrible. Can't I sleep between you? I'm shaking like a leaf.

MAVIS. It was nothing.

PATSY. Just tonight?

MAVIS. You're too big for that kind of thing.

PATSY. Something ought to be done about him.

MAVIS. It was your imagination, it was the wind; it was the shadows.

PATSY. It was Skelly Mannor! I guess I know him when I see him.

MAVIS. Go on back to bed. He's gone.

PATSY. I know I saw him.

MAVIS. Go on, it's okay now; he's gone; whoever it was.

PATSY. Well, it was Skelly Mannor, I guess I know who it was, I saw him.

MAVIS. Something ought to be done about him.

JOSH. He hasn't hurt anyone—not yet.

MAVIS. I suppose you call scaring an innocent girl out of her wits doing nothing. And the whole family too. Everyone knows what he does.

JOSH. Well, what could he do but look? He must be over a hundred if he's a day.

MAVIS. Just looking is doing; who knows what he might do?

JOSH. He's eighty years old.

PATSY. He is not. How can you tell how old he is, through all that filth.

PECK. Well, I know when I was a young man like Josh or younger we used to give old Skelly a "baaa" sometimes——

MAVIS. Peck, now——

PECK. Well, and he looked the same then as he does now, and all the men then said he'd been looking like that for as long as they could remember so he's getting on.

JOSH. He's just a curiosity.

PATSY. Oh, that's very funny. A curiosity. You're just as bright as the sun; you ought to hide your head under a barrel.

JOSH. He's not hurt anybody. Except Warren Peabody.

PATSY. Well, Warren Peabody deserved whatever he got, I'm sure.

MAVIS. What did he do to Warren, is that Laura Peabody's boy?

PATSY. Oh, Lord no; you know he drives an old Chivy, from over at Centerville; part of that river trash bunch. [Exits, coming to LENA.]

JOSH. Well, he hit Warren in the back of the head with a rock, threw it, I'll bet, thirty feet, and caught Warren running. Knocked him out cold.

In town.

LENA [talking to PATSY]. I remember when Driver was alive.

PATSY. Before his accident.

LENA. This was a wonderful place.

PECK [continuing]. He's got a good aim, I can vouch for that.

MAVIS. I've told you, Josh, I don't want you boys teasing him. You just ignore him, I don't care how old you are. I don't know why you do that. You know he could turn on you any second.

JOSH. Oh, I don't bother him.

MAVIS. Well, who knows what's in somebody's mind like that.

On WILMA's *porch.*

WILMA. Like that time he scared young Patsy so bad.

MARTHA. Bad for the whole town with someone like that.

LENA [*to* PATSY]. Like that parade every Saturday afternoon with Driver spinning through town, laughing; I remember his laugh.

PECK. I remember he let Curt Watson have it across the side of the face once. Curt was the fastest runner in town too; let him have it once when Curt gave him a "baaa."

JOSH. God knows he's crazy enough to try to do something like that with a sheep.

MAVIS. Josh, now.

JOSH. Well, I figure maybe he couldn't get a girl.

MAVIS. That's enough.

JOSH. Well, now; the whole town knows what he did; it's not like it was some secret—it's the funniest thing anyone's ever seen around here.

MAVIS. It's not our place to talk.

PECK. I don't imagine he did it much more than once and that time he got caught.

JOSH. That's about the dumbest thing I ever heard. He must have been really hard up is all I can say.

On WILMA's *porch.*

WILMA. To do some bestial thing like that.

MARTHA. When I think of the evil in this world.

LENA [*to* PATSY]. I could just cry.

JOSH. Who saw him?

PECK. Hell, I don't know. It must have been before I was born.

JOSH. Hell, he must be eighty years old.

PECK. Well, he's getting on.

PATSY [*to* LENA]. And Driver Junior. I think he hated his brother. He's just nothing compared. His brother was always so happy at least.

LENA. Driver's been dead now three years tomorrow.

PATSY. May thirty-first.

LENA. Every time I see that car, it just kills me.

JOSH. Some dumb old sheepherder. I hear they're all like that.

PECK. Well, they don't get into town much. Shit, they sure must be hard up is all I can say.

PATSY [to LENA]. His name is Walter, I found out.

JOSH. Shit, I wish I could of seen him. That old son of a bitch. We ought to have him tarred and feathered on Halloween if anyone could find him on Halloween. That old bastard, I don't know how he gets away with the things he does. I know Driver and me was gonna run him out of town once; I think we got drunk instead.

PECK. When was that?

JOSH. Just before his accident sometime. Shit, we used to run that old boy ragged.

PECK. You watch yourself.

MARTHA [to WILMA]. When I think of the evil in this world, I swear.

JOSH. Aw, he hasn't hurt anybody. [He leaves PECK and MAVIS.]

LENA [to PATSY]. I could just cry.

MAVIS. A decent person is afraid to move outside at night; now what kind of life is that?

PECK. Well, we'll tell Clevis and see what he says. He can't do nothing; we didn't catch him at it.

MAVIS. It'll be too late one day and then who's to blame.

The light fades on PECK *and* MAVIS.
Downstairs at the Windrod house.

MARY. I saw it.

NELLY. Sure you did, Mama.

MARY. In my dream. Oh, God; it was horrible, Nelly.

NELLY. Go back to sleep, Mama.

MARY. Someone's going to be butchered in this town. Blood is going to be shed.

NELLY. Be still.

MARY. Blood is going to be shed; someone is going to be butchered.

NELLY. Go on out into your garden, Mama; go back upstairs.

CONGREGATION [softly singing].
       "I walk through the garden alone;
           While the dew is still on the roses . . . [Fading.]

And the voice I hear, falling on my ear—
The prince of peace discloses . . ."

A street.

SKELLY. Hey.

EVA. What? What? What do you want?

SKELLY. You tell him——

EVA. What? I don't know who you're talking about—what do you want?

SKELLY. Your friend.

EVA. Who?

SKELLY. Him. Robert.

EVA. Tell him what?

SKELLY. Tell him he's all right.

EVA. What do you mean he's all right?

SKELLY. He's a good boy.

EVA. Well, I imagine he knows that.

SKELLY. People talk but they don't know—it's them that's the bastards. He's all right.

EVA. You're terrible the way you talk. Nobody makes fun of him. It's you they laugh at.

SKELLY. You tell him . . .

EVA. I don't know what you're talking about. I wouldn't tell anybody anything you told me to tell them.

In the store.

CORA. He drifted in town and he helped around the café for a while and he drifted on; nothing was holding him here.

MARTHA. I heard you started closing the place up at ten in the evening when that boy started working for you.

CORA. When Walter came, yes, I did. I closed earlier. I don't know why I used to be open all that late for anyway.

MARTHA. I heard you still close it up at ten, though.

CORA. Well, force of habit, I suppose.

MARTHA. How long is it he's been gone?

CORA. I don't know, Mrs. Truit; I suppose a month now.

MARTHA. I heard you two made that café a regular show place.

CORA. You'll have to come up sometime and have a cup of coffee and a piece of pie.

MARTHA. Yes, when you was still with your husband, before he left, I mean, I know you used to make the best pie in the state.

CORA. It's still pretty good.

MARTHA [*leaving the store*]. Yes, I will, I'll come up and see you one day. [*To* WILMA.] "Helped around the store," did you ever hear anything like it? I heard she still closes the café at ten sharp. They say he left without taking so much as a stitch she'd bought him. Didn't leave a note even——

In town.

JOSH. I hear Hilltop would be an easy place to break into, if you had in mind to steal something.

MARTHA [*to* WILMA]. Leaves the door for him still, every night.

WILMA. I hear.

MARTHA. Closes at ten.

LENA [*to* JOSH]. That's what I heard.

WILMA. What Reverend Parker said is so true.

MARTHA. Oh, I know it is.

WILMA. It's difficult for us to accept.

MARTHA. "We must accept the blame upon ourselves. Each and every one of us."

WILMA. "It's not Nelly Windrod who is being tried here today."

MARTHA. "Nelly Windrod is not the person who is being tried here today."

WILMA. —No indeed——

PREACHER [*to* CONGREGATION]. —It is the soul and responsibility of our very community. The laxity with which we met the obligations of our Christian lives. The blindness from which we allowed evil in our lives.

CONGREGATION. Amen.

PREACHER. Evil in our lives.

CONGREGATION. Amen.

PREACHER. We watched it fester and grow; we allowed this dreadful thing to happen through shirking our Christian duty. Nelly Windrod——

WILMA. —is not on trial here today.

PREACHER. —No indeed. That man. May the Lord have mercy on his soul. [*Waits.*]

CONGREGATION. Amen.

PREACHER. May the Lord have mercy on his soul and mercy on our blindness to His way. It is our responsibility and we must share in that terrible knowledge.

In town.

LENA. It's not that bad.

PATSY. It's terrible, this crummy old ghost town; tumbleweed blowing down the deserted streets.

LENA. There's no tumbleweed blowing down the——

PATSY. Well, there ought to be, it's enough to give a person the creeps. Everyone from Centerville and all over driving by to see where the murder was committed; it's creepy. Looking at this awful ugly old ghost town, and all the boys know I live here, I swear, I've never been so humiliated in my life.

LENA. I know, it's terrible.

PATSY. Driver Junior never talks to anyone any more—I haven't even seen him with Eva; of course her—that dumb cripple hasn't said a word since. Everyone staring at her—the whole thing is just the ugliest thing I ever heard about. I knew what was going to happen, I said. I swear Driver Junior is such a creep—never spoke to anyone in his life anyway. Doesn't hang around with us or anyone else his own age; hanging around with her, that girl, I feel sorry for her and all, but I look at her and I just feel my shoulder blades start to pooch out all over, people like that—deformed people ought to be put out of sight. Like her and Skelly and everybody; I mean people with deformed minds as well, too; don't think I'm forgetting that. It's absolutely creepy the way people drive through here; I've never been so humiliated in my life.

A street.

SKELLY. You! Hey, Robert. Bobby! Hey!

ROBERT. Hay is for sheep.

SKELLY. Yeah, uh, you, uh—Driver is dead.

ROBERT. Well, I guess I know that.

SKELLY. You going around like——

ROBERT. What? What do you want?

SKELLY. He was a son of a bitch.

ROBERT. Don't talk like that to me.

SKELLY. You don't talk bad.

ROBERT. I don't, no, because I don't see any need to talk——

SKELLY. Driver was a sonabitch. Walking like some kind of stud horse. He wasn't human.

ROBERT. Who are you to tell if someone is human or——

SKELLY. You know what he did? I say. You didn't go to the races to see him kill himself.

ROBERT. My brother was a very good race car driver and I didn't go because I don't like them; if everyone went and I didn't, it's because they like them and I don't.

SKELLY. You don't know. I'll tell you what your sonabitch was like.

ROBERT. You don't know anything.

SKELLY. You hear me talking to people? I *see.* He was a snotnose kid, twelve when you was born. I saw him. And him driving through town like a big shot. With his racing car all green and yellow and rared back there. Lined up after him in cars, trailing after him and honking like a string of geese coming into town.

SKELLY [*continuing*]. And him telling everybody about it up at the café. I heard the stories and the shouting and the glory.

ROBERT. I don't know what you're talking about.

WILMA [*to* MARTHA, *on the latter's porch*]. Land, it was wonderful just to hear them cheering.

MARTHA. Another silver cup, another blue ribbon.

WILMA. First place.

SKELLY. I saw him with Betty Atkins—in her bedroom and her crying and crying and how he hit her—you didn't know that! And she cried 'cause he got so mad. He liked to killed her.

ROBERT. I thought people made up stories about you peeping into windows—you're worse than they say.

SKELLY. I SAW HIM! You're better for a man than he is.

ROBERT. You're disgusting; you're as bad as everybody says you are. Dad says you are and Driver said so too.

SKELLY. Yeah, because I told him I saw him. Your brother, you know what he did? You know what he did? He had to help himself. Had to help himself out. Out in his car parked on the road and in his room. He had to do it for himself.

ROBERT. Shut up!

SKELLY. That's what I know.

ROBERT. You're disgusting. You should be killed or jailed; my brother was a good person; he was a wonderful person.

SKELLY. He beat Betty Atkins and did it by hand. Jacking all on her. I've seen him. I've seen him.

ROBERT. Baaaaaaa.

SKELLY. That's what I know.

ROBERT. You're worse than they say. Everybody knows you spy on them. Who do you think you are?

SKELLY. Who do you think your sonabitch brother was? Is what I want to——

ROBERT. Baaaaaaa. Baaaaaaa.

SKELLY. Now you know! Go on.

ROBERT. BAAAAAAAAA! Baaaaaaaaa.

SKELLY. Get on—get on—Driver Junior, you like that? I know, I know. You like that? Get on. Hey——

ROBERT *exits.*

WILMA. Such a beautiful man; lived so dangerous; like the world wasn't turning fast enough to suit him.

MARTHA. Gave of himself until there was nothing else and got himself killed in an accident.

WILMA. The Lord giveth and the Lord taketh away.

MARTHA. Poor lad. I swear.

Silence. Same street as top of page 27, precisely as before.

SKELLY. Boy! Robert!! Boy! Hey!

EVA. What? What? What do you want?

SKELLY. You tell him——

EVA. What? I don't know who you're talking about—what do you want?

SKELLY. Your friend.

EVA. Who?

SKELLY. Him. Robert.

EVA. Tell him what?

SKELLY. Tell him he's all right.

EVA. What do you mean he's all right?

SKELLY. He's a good boy.

EVA. Well, I imagine he knows that.

SKELLY. People talk but they don't know—it's them that's the bastards. He's all right.

EVA. You're terrible the way you talk. Nobody makes fun of him. It's you they laugh at.

SKELLY. You tell him.

EVA. I don't know what you're talking about. I wouldn't tell anyone anything you told me to tell them.

SKELLY. You tell him . . .

In court.

PECK. We, the jury, find Nelly Windrod. Not guilty.

NELLY [in court]. Oh, God, oh, God. Mama?

JUDGE. It is not Nelly Windrod who is on trial here today.

In town.

PATSY. Tumbleweed blowing through town; it's so creepy I don't know how anyone can stand it.

LENA [to PATSY]. There's no tumbleweed blowing through . . .

On the Windrod porch.

MARY [to EVA]. You talk to him and that's nice. I talk to things too. I talk. I have several tropical fish and a number of small birds that I feed each and every day and take excellent care of them. Talking with them until they die. I like little things, with little hearts beating and little lives around me. Their little hearts just moving away. With short life spans and high temperatures. And I pat out little graves like loaves in the back yard and put little whitewashed gravel, little rocks around each one, and that's my garden. And I decorate the little loaves with flowers when I remember to. Now there's Trinket. That was my rat terrier, died eleven years ago last November, and Bonnie, my cocker spaniel, died four years ago last October, all in the fall; and Gilda and

Wanda, the two goldfish, floating on their sides one morning, little loaves, those two. And Chee-chee, my canary, died two years ago last September. And Goldie, my other canary passed on the year after that and Tina, the little blue kitten—beautiful kitten, that one's little too. She prefers violets and Goldie takes daisies and Chee-chee takes dandelions and Bonnie takes roses, and Trinket has daffodils generally—spring daffodils and Wanda tulips; and the flowers dry up and die and I feel I should bury them too. All my children. Gone, gone, gone.

CONGREGATION [*singing softly*].
> "I walk in the garden alone
> While the dew is still on the roses
> And the voice I hear
> Falling on my ear
> The son of God discloses.
> And he walks with me——"

MARY *and* EVA *join the* CONGREGATION, MARY *by her daughter,* EVA *by her mother.*

CORA [*enters the café from upstairs, sleepily, calling softly as if wakened from sleep*]. Walter?

CONGREGATION. "And he talks with me."

CORA. Walter?

CONGREGATION. "And he tells me I am his own."

CORA. Walter?

CONGREGATION. "And the joy we share."

CORA. Walter!

CONGREGATION. "As we tarry there!"

CORA. Walter!

CONGREGATION. "None other. Has ever——"

CORA. Walter.

CONGREGATION. "Known."

PREACHER. Let us pray.

They bow their heads in silence.

CORA [*falling to her knees as though felled*]. Oh, God. Oh, God. Oh, God. Oh, God. Oh, God. Oh, God. Oh, God.

Curtain.

ACT TWO

On the Johnson porch.

PATSY [*to* LENA]. It wasn't really sudden. I knew he wanted to, he'd let on, you know, in little ways. He said would I mind not being in school; he'll graduate, of course, 'cause this is his last year—and I said would I *mind*?

LENA. That's just incredible; when's it going to be?

PATSY. We aren't messing around; he said two weeks from this Saturday. He didn't want to have a church wedding at first—you know how he is—and I said, Chuck Melton, if you think I'm going to just run off to a preacher and practically elope you got another think coming. So it'll be the First Presbyterian of Centerville, but I want it to be just simple. I said I wanted a street-length dress—I know, but that's what I want and I'll have a veil, a little pillbox hat, I love those, and a veil and probably roses, if it's not too early for roses——

In the Windrod house.

MARY [*over*]. —Bonnie? Here girl. Bonnie? Here kitty, kitty——

LENA. —I'm just so surprised.

PATSY. Well, it wasn't really sudden; I knew he wanted to, he'd let on. I love the First Presbyterian. I only hope the trial and all is quieted down. That could just ruin it all.

LENA. Oh, it will be.

PREACHER [*over*]. Now you know I'm aware we all want to get this settled and go home and forget about it.

PATSY. It's a beautiful church.

LENA. I really love it; it's just beautiful.

PATSY. And my aunt's gonna give the bride's breakfast.

LENA. Aren't you excited?

PATSY. I imagine we'll live in Centerville. You know, till we have enough money to get a place or maybe move somewhere. Probably right in town; there's a wonderful place over the barbershop, the Reganson one on the corner with windows on both sides that's been empty for weeks. I only hope someone doesn't beat us to it. I want to tell Chuck to put some money down on it. I don't want to live with his folks. I just can't stand them and I don't think they think too much of me either. They're so square

34

and old-fashioned. They really are. They don't even smoke or believe in make-up or anything.

LENA. Chuck is wonderful, he really is. I'm just so surprised.

PATSY [*beginning to cry gently*]. He was so cute; he said would I mind not being in school next year, junior year, and I said of course I'll miss my friends, but would I *mind?*

LENA. It's so beautiful. It's a beautiful church for a wedding.

PATSY. Isn't it?

LENA. Aren't you excited? What's wrong?

PATSY. Well, of course I am, silly.

LENA. I don't think Josh and me want to get married, though, until after I'm out of school.

PATSY. Oh, my God, you don't want to marry Josh. My Lord, I can't imagine it. You're not serious about him. Lord, he's so childish.

LENA. He isn't. He's six years older than you are. He's worked for two years.

PATSY. Well, I know, but you don't want to marry him. Age doesn't have anything to do with it. He's all right and he's sweet and all, but I mean to go to the show with and hold hands. I don't know how you can bear to ride into town in that garage tow truck, though.

LENA. I drive it sometimes; it's not bad.

PATSY. Well, I know, but Josh! Lord, Lena, I've got so many things to do yet. You know the thing I think I like most about Chuck is that he's so clean and neat and all. The way he takes care of his Mercury. It's always like spanking new.

In court.

ROBERT. And he took us by surprise.

In the café.

CORA [*to* WALTER]. You seem uneasy.

WALTER. I'm not really.

CORA. I depend on you too much probably.

WALTER. Huh? No, nothing's wrong.

CORA. I've always had a dream, an idea, of maybe leaving here.

WALTER. You have?

CORA. Would you like that?

WALTER. And go where? Hawaii?

CORA. Well, no, not quite Hawaii. I don't know. It's sometimes somewhere and sometimes somewhere else. Somewhere. St. Louis maybe; Des Moines, Chicago. Anywhere.

WALTER. What would you do there?

CORA. The same, of course. Only a nice place maybe. I know the business, if I could sell this place.

WALTER. You wouldn't want to do that, would you?

CORA. Wouldn't you like that? St. Louis maybe, or anywhere. I thought you'd like that. Have a bigger place. Maybe hire someone to run it for us so it doesn't take up all our time.

WALTER. That's an idea. I can't say I like St. Louis much.

CORA. Have you been there? Well, Chicago then.

WALTER. Chicago's nice.

CORA. I have a uncle in Chicago; he might help us get started. What's wrong, anything? You seem uneasy.

WALTER. I'm not. Why don't we close early.

CORA. I'd be agreeable to that.

MARTHA [coming to EVA's porch]. Is she any better?

EVELYN. Oh, I don't know. Who can tell?

SKELLY [entering his shack; alone]. Hound? Hey, hound. What are you shaking about, huh? Get your tail up in the air and out from between your legs like a hunting dog. No, you wouldn't be any good for that, would you? What kind of dog are you? Huh? I got a roast bone from Cora's for you. Here. There you go. Go to it. Those guns scare you, do they? Those hunters? Eh? Oh, they strut around and shoot around after their quail and their duck and their pheasants. They scare you, huh? If you wasn't wild, you could sit out on the steps, huh? No, they'd shoot off one of those duck guns or a firepopper and off you'd go back in under the bed, huh? Under the steps. And they're wasting their shot anyhow. Couldn't hit the broad side of a barn ten feet off. You should have seen it with the mines running. With the mines working and the dynamite and the what-you-call-it booming around everywhere underground fifty times a day or more. Boom! [Laughs.] Boom! [Laughs.] Every hound . . . [Coughs.] . . . every hound in town

kept out of sight from seven in the morning till seven at night.
Under every bed in town. That'd make you shake. Eat it. That's
roast bone. You. [*Laughs.*]

You good for nothing. Oh, hell, yes. They was fancy people;
butter wouldn't melt. Old Man Reiley bought the Eldritch place
up on the hill, wouldn't no other place do for him, and carried
on with their miners drinking parties and societies if you please.
And Glenna Ann sashaying around serving tidbits on a platter;
oh, well-to-do. Blast all day in the mines all day and blast all
night at home. Old Man Reiley called me every name in the
book. Fit to be tied. She was a pretty one, too; only eighteen, the
both of us and her wearing dresses to the ground and bows and
her old man called me every name in the book. Chased me off
the place with a crowbar. [*Laughs.*] And we done it in the old
man's woodshed. Oh, sure. I sneaks back the very same night and
we done it out in the woodshed there. Everything smelling of
hickory and cedar for their fancy fireplaces. Oh, yeah. And, oh,
how she did squirm! Oh, Lord. Saying to me, "Oh, I love you.
Oh, I love you, oh, really I do, Skelly." Oh, shit. [*Coughs.*] Till I
thought she was gonna croak. Oh, Lord. Never let on she even
knew me. Sashsay around town with her big hats. Glenna Ann.
Pretty girl. Oh, yeah. No girl in town so pretty. Then or now.
None in between. How she did claw and bite. No bigger than a
mite. Hound. Where'd you go? Don't you bury that. You eat that
now. That's good. You no good. Old Man Reiley moved off; she
moved off, whole family, lock, stock, and petticoat. Mines give
out, off they git. How she did squirm. "Oh, I love you so much."
Oh, sure. Pretty girl too. Right in the woodhouse the very night
her old man chased me off with a crowbar. And we sat up against
the wall there, playing in the shavings on the floor. Till morning,
near. Sure. All blue. The bluest blue in the morning. Blue light
on her gown there. Sticking her feet into the shavings—digging.
Holding hands, panting. Where's that tea kettle, huh? Where'd it
go? Make some sassafras. Yeah, wouldn't eat it if I gave it to you,
would you? Don't know what's good, do you? Beautiful tits; no
tits like that then or since. I guess you know Peck Johnson fairly
beat the shit out of that girl of his last night. Whipped her good.
Never seen anything like it. Thought she was dead. Patsy. Little
whore she is, too. Thought he near to killed her. The old lady
standing there with her teeth clenched watching, white as a ghost

. . . mad as the devil. Good! I say good! What she done, I say
good! She deserved it; little whore. Here, you whore. Go on with
you! get on out with you. Filthy brother; whole family right along
brother and sister both. Beat her till she nearly bled. Thought he
was gonna kill her. People don't care! What kind of thing goes
on. What kind of devilment. Where'd you go to? Hound? What-
are-you-not eating? If you was tame, you could come out and sit
on the street. Catch a rabbit, huh? You scared of rabbits? Are
you? That's a good girl. You're okay. Bluest blue you ever saw in
the daytime. Cold too and her in a nightgown; run right off of the
house when I called up and off we went. [*Laughs.*] Oh, boy! Arms
is no good. Can't lift 'em even over my head. Look a-there. Oh,
boy. Red thing over her nightgown there. Barefoot. Grass sticking
to her feet from the fresh-cut lawns with their lackeys there, mow-
ing and clipping and futsing. Barefoot. Right across the dew and
all.

That crippled girl, Jackson, she's got her leg shorter, one than
the other. Cries. You never saw anything like it. Dances around
her room in the window curtains, all lace, wrapped around her
whooping, dancing around like a banshee. Oh, he's all right. Tell
him I said he's all right. Well, I guess he knows that. No, he
don't know it, now, there! Better'n his no good brother everybody yelling about doing it by hand. Hitting girls around. People don't care! They don't see. What. What they want to think
they think; what they don't they don't. They don't care anyway;
what kind of devilment. What goes on. Her old man, Old Man
Reiley; never did know. No, no. Never did know. I weren't the
only one either, you can bet. Get some water boiling; make some
sassafras; good for the stomach. Cedar. All in the air. Bluest blue
in the air. Hickory and cedar cedar cedar cedar cedar in the air.
Sang. [*Laughs.*] All manner of songs there. Soft so's it wouldn't
carry to the lackeys' house there. Carrying on, scratching, biting,
thought she was gonna croak. "Oh, really, oh, I love you so!"
[*Laughs.*] Pretty girl. Beautiful tits. Beautiful tits. Oh, yes. Oh,
sure.

On Eva's *porch.*

MARTHA. Is she any better?

EVELYN. Oh, I don't know. Who can tell?

MAVIS. Has she said anything?

EVELYN. The doctor said it was just shock.

MARTHA. Well, I'd think so.

WILMA. I've never heard anything like it.

MARTHA. Like when he scared young Patsy so bad.

WILMA. Bad for the whole town.

MAVIS. It's awful.

PATSY. I feel so sorry for her.

WILMA. How's Driver Junior?

EVELYN. He hasn't been over. I don't know what to think about that. I'd told her not to go off; well, I won't say anything.

MARTHA. Such a shock. For us all.

MAVIS. A terrible thing.

EVELYN. She's always been so easily upset.

LENA. Well, she has cause.

PATSY. I just wish he was still alive! That's what I wish.

WILMA. When I think of the evil in this world.

EVELYN. The doctor said she just needs rest.

MAVIS. If he'd of lived he'd not have seen the light of day tomorrow.

WILMA. That poor girl.

MARTHA. And Nelly, that poor woman, the life that woman leads.

WILMA [leaving]. I said to Eva's mother—cried the whole time——

MARTHA. I know, I saw——

WILMA. Only God in His Heaven.

In court.

MARY. It appeared to me that both the men were hitting at her.

Tremendous crowd reaction.

JUDGE. Order!

MARY. It appeared to me.

JUDGE. Now you have testified, as a witness, Mrs. Windrod.

MARY. I was at my window, watching the moon.

ROBERT [to MARY, *but not in court*]. Was there a moon?

MARY. A crescent moon that night, I know for sure.

JUDGE. You have testified that you saw——

MARY. Blood, everywhere; all over. It was terrible. On the porch, rivers and I was mopping and it spread with the water, all around, all over.

JUDGE. —Driver Junior and young Eva clearly.

MARY. I didn't say "clearly," I couldn't see clearly; I don't see well.

JUDGE. You testified you saw——

MARY. In my dream.

JUDGE. You were asleep?

MARY. Weeks ago and I told Nelly that blood was going to be shed, and I was wiping and it spread with the water, all around on the porch—— [*She leaves the stand.*]

NELLY [*taking the stand*]. And Mama said someone was in the back yard and I took up the gun that I keep by the door, the shotgun; and checked to see if it was loaded and it was and I opened the door.

MARY [*over*]. —Bonnie? Here, kitty, kitty, here, girl.

In the café.

CORA [*to* WALTER]. Did you go into town?

WALTER. Yeah.

CORA. Into Centerville?

WALTER. No, no, only into Eldritch.

CORA. Did you? Well, what do you think?

WALTER. Well, what can I tell you, it's a ghost town.

CORA. I told you.

WALTER. What was that big building?

CORA. The movie house?

WALTER. On the corner.

CORA. Oh, there was a drugstore, and an exchange. And a lawyer's office and a couple of doctors up above had their office in that building. A dentist, I think. That was the first building to shut down.

WALTER. Some people said hello like they knew me.

CORA. Well, they do know you from here.

WALTER. Wonder what they think?

CORA. You do, do you?

WALTER. Sometimes.

CORA. Peck Johnson said the new boy "helping" me appeared to be a genuine good worker.

WALTER. What did you say to that?

CORA. Well, I said, oh, yes, yes, he's a genuine good worker.

WALTER [*laughing*]. I like some of them all right. The truck drivers are all right, anyway.

CORA. Oh, they're from all over; they support the place. Have for years.

WALTER. Some of the people from Eldritch aren't so bad.

CORA. I think a couple of the girls have a crush on you. Well, I don't blame them.

WALTER. They're young.

CORA. Well, they're not all that damn young.

WALTER. It's gonna be a nice night.

CORA. It's gonna be a nice summer.

> JOSH *and the* TRUCKER *walk casually to* SKELLY.

EVA [*in the woods*]. No, in the wintertime and in the autumn especially. It's so nice; it smells so clean.

ROBERT [*in court*]. He came from nowhere!

EVELYN [*on her porch*]. I said she shouldn't be out gone from the house like that!

JOSH [*to* SKELLY]. What are you standing on the corner about? Why aren't you back to your grubby house? Where do you sleep now your stinking shack burned down? Or do you sleep? Do you sleep? Sleep with sheep, huh?

SKELLY. Get on.

TRUCKER. What'd you say?

SKELLY. Mind your own business.

JOSH. Which old damp rotting cellar do you haul up in now your dry old shack's gone? Huh? I bet you eat worms, doncha.

SKELLY. Go on, you.

JOSH. What d'you eat? Won't tell anybody where you live, will you? 'Cause you know what'd happen if you closed your eyes there, don't you?

SKELLY. Yeah, you sonabitch, you mind your own—I don't say whether I got ary a bed or no now.

JOSH. What'd you call me?

SKELLY. Go on with you.

JOSH. I said what'd you call me?

TRUCKER. Ought to kill him, Josh.

JOSH. What'd you say? Shit, he ain't worth it.

SKELLY. Get on.

JOSH. Just don't let anybody follow you home. [SKELLY *leaves.*] You get on now. You're the one who had better get on, not me. You'll wake up to a hot bed one of these days again. [*Laughs.*] Old bastard. BAAAAA! [*Laughs.*]

TRUCKER. Son of a bitch shepherd!

In court.

ROBERT. He was just there all of a sudden from nowhere and he took us by surprise and he pushed me—he hit me from behind; I don't know if I passed out or not. [*Crowd murmur.*] He's immensely strong. [*Crowd murmur.*]

MARY [*overlapping crowd murmur, in her house*]. Nelly, Nelly, there's someone out back, honey, having a terrible fight. They came through the woods and started yelling all kinds of things.

NELLY [*to* MARY]. Where was you? I thought you was in bed.

ROBERT. And I heard a ringing in my ears and I saw what he was trying to do and everything went white. [*Crowd reaction.*] And he pushed me! [*Crowd reaction.*]

MARY. You better go out and see, honey.

PATSY [*to* LENA; *in town*]. I mean he's out there polishing the chrome and dash and all.

LENA. I know, it's amazing.

Some of the crowd reaction has been to EVA, *who has been moaning throughout* ROBERT'S *testimony. Now she screams—a huge ear-splitting scream, and I mean it.*

EVELYN. Oh, God, baby, my baby——

EVA. —No, no, no, no, no!——

EVELYN. See her crippled body. See her broken back; why, why has God cursed me with this burden. I don't complain. I ask why?

We love Him. We bless Him. Praise Him. And this monster! I mean Skelly! My daughter is weak; you're trying to kill her! Look at her! Is that what you want? I only ask why?

PREACHER [*overlapping*]. The Lord works in——

EVELYN [*overlapping*]. WHY? I said, why? I have a right to know; I'll repent if I've done anything; if I've sinned——

CORA [*overlapping*]. —Eva said to me—Eva, you know what you said. Skelly worked for me sometimes; none of you knew him. He was honest.

EVELYN [*overlapping*]. My daughter has never spoken to you; my daughter has never spoken to a person like you; my daughter has been scarred, permanently scarred by this. She's crippled already. She's weak. She can't stand up.

CORA. If you'd listen to me.

EVELYN. No, no. I won't listen to you; I won't trust the word of a woman like you.

CORA. And what are you?

Crowd reaction, which continues until singing begins.

EVELYN [*screaming wildly*]. My daughter is a virgin! She's pure! She's a Christian, from a Christian home; a daughter of God and you'd put your word against the word of a virgin. A beer-swilling harlot. Everyone knows. A drunken Whore of Babylon! Harlot! Daughter of Babylon! Go back to your beer parlor; your house of sin. You couldn't keep your husband and you couldn't keep your whore boy friend. In the name of God before this court I call you that. Liar. You're the liar. Before God I call you that. On His word. His holy word. Yes! Put her on the stand. Let her

CORA. I talked to her because I knew Skelly would never, *never* harm anyone. If you'd listen to me.

JUDGE [*begins pounding steadily with the gavel*]. Order. Order. Order. Order.

The CONGREGATION *begins singing "When the Roll Is Called Up Yonder," to the rhythm of the gavel. The* CONGREGATION *drowns* EVELYN *out with the loud, joyous hymn, the pulpit beaten now, in time to the song. The song is sung to its finish. Everyone moves into small groups. Worried, quiet.*

talk. We have nothing to hide.
Ask her if she didn't keep a
whore boy friend up to her
place. Ask her what kind of
woman she is. . . .

A long pause. Silence.

PATSY [*very upset; quietly to* WALTER]. Pretty sure.

WALTER [*beside her, after a pause*]. Are you sure it's me? [*Pause.*] You're not sure are you? [*Pause.*] It could be somebody else. It could have been what's-his-name. Chuck. [*Pause.*]

PATSY. Well, it was somebody! [*Pause.*] Oh, God.

WALTER. I don't know what you want from me.

PATSY. I'll tell your precious Cora what you're like. Then we'll see how high and mighty you think you are. No, you wouldn't like that very much, would you?

A street in town: the JUDGE, PECK, *the* TRUCKER, *and* JOSH *in a group. They speak with deliberation.*

JUDGE. The oats was late 'cause of the spring was so wet.

PECK. Me and the boy couldn't plant till late May. Eighteenth of May. Up till then the ground was so wet we couldn't get at the field even.

TRUCKER. And then that cold spell.

JUDGE. Ground was solid out our way till almost April.

JOSH. Hell it was.

JUDGE. Almost April. You couldn't stick a fork into it. Hard as a rock.

PECK. 'Course you're high; it wasn't near so bad along in the valley.

TRUCKER. Oh, no. It wasn't near.

PECK. Along the valley there I don't imagine there was more than six-ten cold days. Days it was froze solid. River wasn't more than three inches ice.

JOSH. I don't believe it ever froze clear across.

PECK. No, it never froze across.

JOSH. There was some running out aways right through the winter.

PECK. 'Course you're up on the hill there. You're not protected.

TRUCKER. Yeah, it was froze solid right up through April.

JUDGE. 'Course the rains was bad for you. In the valley there.

JOSH. Oh, yeah.

TRUCKER. I don't believe I've ever seen the rains so bad.

PECK. Yeah, the river swelled up there along in March, I can't remember it that bad before. I said to Josh, I couldn't remember it that bad. There was that.

JOSH. Most of the field was under six-ten feet of water along in the spring.

PECK. April it was.

JOSH. Yeah, I believe it was April.

PECK. Wasn't able to set a plow till late in the month. Plowed for the oats finally in May. Eighteenth of May; that's the latest I can remember. I believe it was the eighteenth.

JOSH. It was, I remember.

PECK. Latest I remember.

JUDGE. Well, you're in the valley there; you're not protected.

TRUCKER. The floods was bad for you.

PECK. Yeah, I'll say. It's rich soil, though. Good bottom topsoil.

TRUCKER. Yeah, it's rich bottom land.

PECK. It's good bottom land.

TRUCKER. It's good for corn.

PECK. Oh, yeah.

JUDGE. It's sandy for oats though.

JOSH. Yeah, the oats idn't doing well.

TRUCKER. Well, it's been dry the past month.

PECK. Radio says we might be heading for a drought.

JUDGE. I been thinking I might have to irrigate. Later on. If it doesn't get wetter.

JOSH. Yeah, we had all our rains right there together.

TRUCKER. Not what you'd call a deep rain though.

JUDGE. No, it run right off, much as there was of it. Could sure use some of it now.

PECK. Oh, yeah.

JUDGE. The corn's beginning to curl; I noticed this morning.

JOSH *leaves, goes to* LENA's *porch.*

TRUCKER. It was dry this morning. Almost no dew even.

PECK. There wasn't much even low like I am. Course you're up on the hill. You must be getting the worst of it.

JOSH [to LENA]. Just got off work.

LENA. You look it; you didn't even wash up.

JOSH. I did, but it'll have to wear off; it's ground right in, I think.

LENA. Where did you want to go tonight?

JOSH. You mind eating up at Cora's or you want to go into Centerville?

LENA. It doesn't matter, whatever you want.

JOSH. We might as well go on into town to the drive-in.

LENA. Oh lets, 'cause Patsy'll be there and I wanted to see her.

JOSH. You've seen her this morning.

LENA. Yes, but she said she had a surprise she wanted to tell me.

JOSH. I don't know what she thinks is a surprise. Then we'll go into the movies, all right? Or would you rather just drive?

LENA. I'd kinda like to see the picture.

JOSH. Whatever you want.

LENA [going to PATSY]. She's gonna be with Chuck so you be nice to him.

PATSY. Don't you think he's cute, though?

LENA. I guess.

PATSY. Was he really at the drive-in with her? That's so funny. His name's Walter I found out. But I can't imagine. That's the funniest thing; I just wish I'd have seen it.

LENA. It's not so bad.

PATSY. But, she's so old for him. My God, she's thirty-eight.

LENA. She isn't, is she? Mama said thirty-four.

PATSY. Well, she's older than any thirty-four, and besides that's bad enough.

LENA. That soldier you went out with last year was that old.

PATSY. He was not.

LENA. I'll bet he was. He was balding.

PATSY. He was not, what do you think I am, he had a crew cut; besides he was twenty-six, I saw his ID.

LENA. Oh, he wasn't any twenty-six.

PATSY. I saw his draft card, Lena. Besides, my God, it's different with a boy. He was very nice. Besides, I only went out with him twice. I felt sorry for him. We didn't do anything.

On EVA's porch.

CORA. That's hard for me to believe, Eva.

EVA. You ask Robert; what difference does it make?

CORA. 'Cause he worked for me; he used to pick up the garbage for his hogs. He lived out back of the café for years, till they burned that shack down. I still say it was Driver Junior's brother and Josh did it, burned that shack down.

EVA. We come into the clearing back behind Nelly Windrod's house, by her mill there, and I heard something, and he said he'd show me what.

CORA. Skelly did? He did not.

EVA. No. He didn't say.

CORA. Eva if that's not the truth, you better say how it really happened.

EVA. I said it happened like Robert said. It's like that and I don't care if you knew him or not. Mama said the preacher said a sermon about the evil in people like him and that we should have killed him or something before he had a chance to take advantage of me. I've been cursed and scarred.

CORA. You can't lie under oath, Eva.

EVA [*running away*]. You're the one who's going to hell. Not me. I didn't do it, anyway; Nelly did it.

In the café.

CORA. It wasn't Skelly.

TRUCKER [*leaving café*]. Well, who do you think it was?

CORA. She told me.

TRUCKER. If he hadn't of died, I know he wouldn't have seen the light of day the next morning. [*Goes to* JOSH.]

A street in town.

JOSH [*almost good-naturedly*]. Damn that mutt anyway.

TRUCKER. Good watchdog, is he?

JOSH. That old bitch of a dog, I'll kill that bitch.

TRUCKER. Wakes up the folks does he?

JOSH. Every damn time we drive up it starts up a racket. Son of a
bitch, every light in the house goes on. She has to run on in, the
noise that dog raises, every goddamned night. I don't care how
easy I drive up. We started parking on down the block, she still
starts up as soon as Lena steps a foot on the porch.

On MARTHA's porch.

MARTHA. When I think of the evil in this world.

WILMA. To do some bestial thing like that.

In town.

PECK [*to the* TRUCKER *and the* JUDGE]. Well, I never figured him to
actually hurt anybody.

TRUCKER. Hell, we all knew he was loony.

JUDGE. Someone like that—we all knew he was capable of any kind
of thing.

PECK. Capable, yes, but I never figgered him for actually hurting
anybody.

TRUCKER. Well, when somebody lives like that—away from everybody.

PECK. The boys give him a hard time but he can take care of himself.

TRUCKER. Should have been put away the way he looks at everybody.

JUDGE. Should have been shot—just shot in the woods; nobody the
wiser.

PECK. I just never really figgered him to do anything. Capable, yes,
but I have to admit I'd never thought he'd do anything. Outright,
I mean.

MARTHA [*on her porch*]. Why, she called Evelyn Jackson a liar to
her face, and Eva too. Swore things, the devil and his angels
wouldn't believe it. She'd stand up there and swear black was
white.

MARY [*in her house, upstairs*]. Nelly, Nelly, there's someone out
back, honey, having a terrible fight; they came through the woods
and started yelling all kinds of things.

NELLY [*as she exits to a street in town*]. Where was you? I thought you was in bed.

MARY. You better go out and see, honey.

MAVIS. Morning.

NELLY. Good morning.

MAVIS. We don't see you to talk to much.

NELLY. Well, summer is a slow time; I've been saving up strength for Peck's corn crop this year.

MAVIS. It's sure looking good.

NELLY. I drive past; I've been keeping my eye on it.

MAVIS. How is the mill?

NELLY. Well, summer is slow.

MAVIS. We see you drive by.

NELLY. Evenings I've been going into Centerville; talking to the farmers over there; say we might be into a drought.

MAVIS. We saw you, I believe going into the movie house there.

NELLY. Yes, I don't get a chance to go often.

MAVIS. Well, we don't go.

NELLY. I've seen the girl there.

MAVIS. Patsy? Oh, yes, Patsy enjoys it. She goes with Chuck; awfully nice boy; I guess you know we're planning a wedding; I said it wasn't any use having a church wedding, all amounts to the same —Patsy wouldn't hear of it, of course, so I suppose we're going all out.

NELLY. He's an awfully nice boy, I hear.

MAVIS. Do you? I'm glad to hear it; we hardly know them really; but he does seem sweet; his family has a lovely farm, we visited. Last Sunday. They grow up so fast.

NELLY. Quite a nice young lady.

MAVIS. We're proud of her. How's your mother?

NELLY. Oh, Mom's the same; her mind's gone. I hate to leave her alone nights. Just like a child.

MAVIS. Well, you have a life of your own; you have to get out.

NELLY. Yes, I do. I hate to leave her, though, just the same.

MAVIS. We see you driving into Centerville.

NELLY. It's good to get away from the mill; Duane nearly runs it for me now.

MAVIS. I was talking to your mother; poor thing.

NELLY. Yes, it's sad.

MAVIS. I remember she had a fine mind.

NELLY. Yes, she did. One of the first registered nurses in Des Moines. Long time ago now; when she was a girl.

MAVIS. She goes on terrible about you; poor thing.

NELLY. I know, she doesn't know what she's saying half the time.

MAVIS. Still she tells things; it must be terrible for you.

NELLY. I'll take care of her, Mavis, as long as my strength holds out.

MAVIS. Martha Truit said, the life you have to bear.

NELLY. It's my cross, Mavis.

MAVIS. I know, I told Peck . . .

NELLY. How is Peck?

MAVIS. Oh, he's all right; his back is giving him trouble again. It's just nerves I keep telling him, but I don't know. Between you and me I don't know.

On MARTHA's porch.

WILMA. Who knows what's in somebody's mind like that.

MARTHA. Like that time—when was it, last summer.

The people have wandered to random, scattered positions about the stage. They stand still and isolated, ROBERT and EVA moving about them as though walking through the woods.

EVA. No, in the wintertime and in the autumn. It's so nice, it smells so clean.

ROBERT. Okay, the fall then.

EVA. Yes. And it's heavy, heavy frost and it covers everything and that's rime.

ROBERT. And it's just frost? Is it a hoarfrost?

EVA. That's it, hoarfrost is rime. And it covers everything. Every little blade of grass and every tree and houses and everything. Like it's been dipped in water and then in sugar.

ROBERT. Or salt. Yeah, I know what it is.

EVA. It's better than ice storms or anything like that. And everything is white and sparkling so clean when the sun comes up it nearly blinds you and it's rare! It doesn't happen every year. And that's what I'd like to be. What I'd like to do. I have a book with a picture of Jack Frost painting rime on a windowpane with a paintbrush. Do you fly? Do you dream you fly?

ROBERT. When?

EVA. Ever?

ROBERT. I guess. I haven't thought about it.

EVA. How high? Think about it. It's important. Everybody flies, it's important how high.

ROBERT. I don't know. Just over the ground.

EVA. Really?

ROBERT. I guess. As high as my head. I'm always getting tangled up in wires and all.

EVA. I'm way over the treetops, just over the treetops, just brushing against the treetops, and I fly right over them, just brush them with my arms out. Over the whole town like an airplane. Spreading this salt frost in the autumn. I love autumn. And when the sun comes up——

ROBERT. Right.

EVA. It'll blind you!

ROBERT. I've seen it.

EVA. It's so bright it blinds you. I want to fly like that, all over the town, right over everybody. It's beautiful. [SKELLY *takes a step forward, among the silent people.*] Listen! Listen! Did you hear something?

The people move from their still positions into small groups. SKELLY *comes to* CORA *and* WALTER.

CORA. Are you out there?

SKELLY. Here. Yeah.

CORA. Can Walter help you? You know Walter.

SKELLY. Yeah, I know.

CORA. We're gonna be turning in, but he can help you with it.

SKELLY. The white one, with the spots?!

CORA. Spotty?

SKELLY. Had a litter.

CORA. She did?

SKELLY. She had four but she ate one.

CORA. Skelly, you just let them go wild, that's terrible; you should take them away from her.

SKELLY. The runt, the last one.

WALTER. She what? She ate one of them?

CORA. Pigs do that sometimes; they're terrible. A runt or something that they think is weak, they will.

WALTER. Couldn't you stop her?

SKELLY. I didn't see it.

CORA. Oh, he lets them just go wild, you can't get near them; one of them's all right, the brown one.

SKELLY. She's good.

CORA. One of them is tame and nice, the rest you can't get near them. He has four. So that makes seven now, doesn't it? You're getting to be a regular rancher.

SKELLY. The brown's a good one.

CORA. He has an old hound dog he keeps too; he's good with them but they just run wild. [*She leaves.*]

WALTER. You want me to help you?

SKELLY. I'm all right. You like her?

WALTER. Do I like? What? Who?

SKELLY. Jackson. [*Pause.*] That Patsy Jackson. Cora ain't good to you?

WALTER. Cora? I imagine she's good to everybody.

SKELLY. But you. She's good to you. I seen you with Patsy Jackson. You like her? You like that carrying on?

WALTER. What? I thought you were talking about your brown sow; I've not seen her.

SKELLY. I said, if you think you're a big man and you play around here and you play around there.

WALTER. You want me to help you slop the hogs?

SKELLY. I'll be all right.

WALTER. Well, if you make it your business to know what everybody is doing, I see why Cora makes sure we pull down the shades at night, and turn off the light and listen to hear if anyone's about. If that's your business, I guess I don't have to tell you what Patsy Jackson is like.

SKELLY. She's a bitch.

WALTER. Patsy? And them that lies down with . . .

SKELLY. Cora's a good woman.

WALTER. Yes, well, you slop the hogs and carry off the garbage and I build the fence and paint the café; we're none of us freeloaders, I don't suppose. I don't imagine I owe anyone anything except money. I don't owe anybody time. I can't say that I see it as any of your business anyway, Skelly. You don't have to worry about her; she's managed seven years without you or me either. Don't you think? [*Pause.*] Wouldn't you say? [*Pause.*] You go on and slop your hogs. [*Pause.*] Go on, get on, be thankful she gives it to you for the price of carrying it away. [*Pause.*] Hey. What do you do with those hogs anyway? How come they're so wild? [*Pause.*]

SKELLY. I feed 'em, they run wild.

WALTER. Go on, I didn't mean anything by it. Good night.

MARY [*to* MAVIS]. I have a bruise there on the inside of my elbow, she holds onto me there, she pushes at me terrible, she can't help it.

A street in town.

EVA. If you had a car, you could drive all over.

ROBERT. What do I want with a car?

EVA. Are you afraid?

ROBERT. What for? So I can drive around the square. Around the square, around the square. It's all they ever do; all the boys with cars. Around the square and over into Centerville to a drive-in to eat and a drive-in to see a movie.

EVA. You just don't want to be like——

ROBERT. Everybody doesn't have to have a car. Everybody talks like that's all there is. The guys at school spend their whole lives in or on top of or under their cars. They eat in them and sleep in them and change clothes and drink and get sick and vomit and make out with their girls—it's all they even ever talk about. Evolution's gonna take their feet right away from them. Make turtles with wheels for legs out of them.

Eva. I think you're just afraid 'cause of Driver.

Robert. Well, that's another thing I hadn't thought of. They die in them too. Live and die without ever stepping outside. Why would I want that?

Lena [*offstage*]. Sometimes I think life is so short and we should enjoy it for the time we're here and then I think I should work really hard so I can be comfortable, you know, after I've made some money, and then I think how awful working all that time would be and most of my life would be gone by that time and I'd have wasted it, you know what I mean? No, no, don't, Josh!

Josh [*offstage, to* Lena]. You said you would.

Lena. Sometime, I said.

Josh. You don't want to?

Lena. It isn't that. You know. Don't now!

Josh. What?

Lena. You know. If something happens, you don't know what can happen. And there's no assurance—of what can happen.

Josh. Nothing can happen, I told you.

Lena. Come on. Don't now! I'm not kidding now.

Josh. Just see.

Lena. You don't like me really or you'd respect me.

Josh. What? I don't like you? Why do you think I want to?

Lena. You know what I mean.

Josh. Just see. Just see. Just see. Nothing will happen; just see.

Lena. No, I said, now. Come on.

Josh. Jesus Christ, Lena.

Lena. Well, don't be mad.

Josh. Well, you let me go so far and then say no, I don't know what you expect.

Lena. It's all right, isn't it? Josh? Well, don't just sit there. I said sometime. Sometime, really. I mean it. Just not tonight. Okay? I want to, too; I just said not tonight. Really. It just scares me. Okay? Okay? [*Pause. Then rapidly.*] Josh! Damn it, now, come on. No! I said and that means no! Good Lord. [*Sound of someone being slapped. Pause.*] Now you're mad, aren't you?

Preacher [*to* Congregation]. No, sir, it is the soul and responsibility of our very community. The laxity with which we met the obligations of our Christian lives. The blindness from which we allowed evil in our lives. We watched it fester and grow; we allowed this dreadful thing to happen through shirking our Christian duty. Nelly Windrod is not on trial here today. That man, may the Lord have mercy on his soul damned eternally to hell, and our blindness to His way. It is our responsibility and we must share that terrible knowledge. As you go your ways tonight. As you leave and walk and drive to your homes, realize that the burden must be ours and ask the Lord for his grace. Pray for these two souls as you pray for the lost, the outcast, as you pray for the soul of the damned, and the care of our boys overseas; Pray to the Lord to unlock the bitterness in the hearts of those like him in the world today and pray that they may see the light of His holy way.

CONGREGATION. Amen.

PREACHER. Amen, the Lord be with you.

The CONGREGATION *walks slowly, as if coming from church, to the positions of the woods.*

JOSH. Had the Olds out last night.

TRUCKER. The old man's Olds?

JOSH. Took it out onto the Old Sparta Road and opened it up.

TRUCKER. Gene was out there last week.

JOSH. Pegged it. Hundred twenty. That old needle was bouncing against the peg and half the way back again. Two miles or over, then I eased it down.

TRUCKER. We'll have to take 'em out Sunday.

In the woods—precisely as before, a rerun.

EVA. And it covers everything and that's rime.

ROBERT. And it's just frost? Is it a hoarfrost?

EVA. That's it, hoarfrost is rime. And it covers everything. Every little blade of grass and every tree and houses and everything. Like it's been dipped in water and then in sugar.

ROBERT. Or salt. Yeah, I know what it is.

EVA. It's better than ice storms or anything like that. And everything is white and sparkling so clean when the sun comes up it nearly blinds you and it's rare! It doesn't happen every year. And that's what I'd like to be. What I'd like to do. I have a book with a picture of Jack Frost painting rime on a windowpane with a paintbrush. Do you fly? Do you dream you fly?

ROBERT. When?

EVA. Ever?

ROBERT. I guess. I haven't thought about it.

They walk about the forest, walking slowly through the people.

EVA. How high? Think about it. It's important. Everybody flies, it's important how high.

ROBERT. I don't know. Just over the ground.

EVA. Really?

ROBERT. I guess. As high as my head. I'm always getting tangled up in wires and all.

EVA. I'm way over the treetops, just over the treetops, just brushing against the treetops, and I fly right over them, just brush them with my arms out. Over the whole town like an airplane. Spreading this salt frost in the autumn. I love autumn. And when the sun comes up——

ROBERT. Right.

EVA. It'll blind you!

ROBERT. I've seen it.

EVA. It's so bright it blinds you. I want to fly like that, all over the town, right over everybody. It's beautiful. [SKELLY *steps forward.*] Listen! Listen. Did you hear something?

ROBERT. No. What?

EVA. Like something rustling in the leaves?

ROBERT. No. What? It was probably a rabbit.

SKELLY steps forward again.

EVA. Listen.

ROBERT. I don't hear anything.

EVA. Maybe it was the wind.

ROBERT. There isn't any; maybe it was a fox.

EVA. Don't.

ROBERT. Or a wolf.

EVA. Ted Caffey trapped a wolf in his barn last year.

ROBERT. Shot its head off too.

EVA. Oh, he did not—are you trying to scare me?—it got away.

ROBERT. Shot it and killed it; took its pelt into the county agent in Centerville and got twenty dollars for it.

EVA. It wasn't anything; we better get back.

ROBERT. It was probably the mate looking for the one Caffey shot.

EVA. Don't say that, it wasn't—— [SKELLY *moves again.*] Listen!

ROBERT. It wasn't anything.

They stop still.

WALTER [*turning from his tree position*]. What's that junk heap of a what was it a Plymouth?

CORA. At Church Street? That's Driver's car. Driver Junior's older brother. Drove it in stock car races; over in Centerville they have a track. The whole town went; used to, when he drove. I suppose they think it's bad luck now, he had some kind of accident; smashed it to hell, it looks like, doesn't it?

WALTER. He get killed?

CORA. Oh, yes, killed instantly. They hitched up a chain to the car and pulled it back here.

WALTER. And dumped it in the middle of the street? The grass and weeds almost cover it; I didn't know what it was at first.

CORA. Well, that's where the chain broke and the axle broke and every other damn thing broke, so there it sits. Not a very pretty sight.

They move a few steps.

The following is from all over the stage. The characters may move from their stationary positions for a few steps and return to them. The woods become alive with their voices. The sequence should begin softly and build, becoming faster and more forceful toward the end.

MARY. Rusting away—flaking away.

EVELYN. Falling apart, boarded together, everything flapping and rusting.

MARY. All the buildings bowing and nodding.

PATSY. Movie house been closed down eight years.

TRUCKER. It was dry this morning; almost no dew even.

NELLY. You fall down, you bruise, you run into things, you're old.

PATSY. Tumbleweed blowing down the deserted streets.

MARY. And the flowers dry up and die.

SKELLY. You didn't go to the races to see him kill himself.

EVA. And it covers everything and that's rime.

LENA. I remember his laugh.

CORA. Eldritch is all but a ghost town.

WILMA. The wages of sin——

MARTHA. I don't know, love.

EVA. And when the sun comes up it blinds you!

EVELYN. The mine shaft building used to just shine.

SKELLY. All in the air.

JOSH. Just see.

LENA. It's a beautiful church.

WALTER. Wouldn't you say?

MAVIS. A decent person is afraid to move outside at night.

PREACHER. As you go your way tonight.

CORA. You seem uneasy.

EVELYN. The doctor said it was just shock.

PECK. You watch yourself.

MARY. Gone, gone gone.

EVA. Like it's been dipped in water and then in sugar.

MAVIS. And not seen the light of day tomorrow.

MARY. All my children.

EVA. And that's what I want to be.

They are still, trees again.

MARY. Gone, gone gone.

EVA [*continuing, in the woods*]. You know what my mother says?

ROBERT. What?

EVA. When I come in?

ROBERT. What?

EVA. She says you're unresponsible, and she asks me things like where we go and all, everywhere we go every time I go anywhere with you. Everything we do.

ROBERT. Where does she think we go?

EVA. Oh, I tell her we just go walking in the woods; talking. She knows that but she thinks we do other things too.

ROBERT. Like what?

EVA. You know.

ROBERT. Like what?

EVA. You know. Dirty things.

ROBERT. What does she think that for?

EVA. I don't tell her, though.

ROBERT. What would you tell her?

EVA. About that. About when I have to pee and things.

ROBERT. Well, there's nothing dirty about that.

EVA. Well, don't you think I know!

ROBERT. She means other things.

EVA. What?

ROBERT. Never mind.

EVA. Well, don't you think I know? I know. You don't do things like that, you don't even look! I can, though; I know.

ROBERT. You don't know anything.

EVA. I DO TOO! I've seen. You think I'm so young because I'm so little. I'm fourteen; I can have babies already; and I've seen cows do it when they're in heat. But you wouldn't do something like that.

ROBERT. Let's go back.

EVA. Let's do. I know how; I can.

ROBERT. When cows are in heat, that's one cow jumping on another; you don't know anything.

EVA. You're ashamed; you're not old enough to.

ROBERT. You don't know what you're talking about.

EVA. Boys have to be older. But I'll bet your brother could anyway. I might as well because she thinks we do anyway. You're the one who doesn't know anything about it.

ROBERT. I should, just to show you—don't—you don't know what you're talking about.

EVA. What?

ROBERT. Anything. Because you don't know anything about it.

EVA. I do too. You're afraid.

ROBERT. You don't know what you're talking about even.

Their lines begin to overlap.

EVA. Only not here.

ROBERT. Why not? What's wrong with here?

EVA. You have to be in bed, stupid!

ROBERT. If you think you know so much. [*Grabbing her.*]

EVA [*violently*]. Let go of me! You leave me alone. I will if I want to.

ROBERT. You want to get it in you so bad! You think I can't.

EVA. Stop it.

ROBERT. You think I won't do it.

EVA. Leave me alone. I'll tell.

ROBERT. No you won't; you asked for it.

EVA. Leave me alone.

ROBERT [*throwing her to the ground*]. You think you're so smart; I'll show you. Shut up now, shut up or I'll kill you anyway; you asked for it. [*They struggle violently on the ground. Eva saying, "No, stay away, leave me alone," screaming.*] You little whore; you think I won't. Stop it.

SKELLY [*from the woods, breaking toward them. His lines are simultaneous with the above struggle*]. What do you think —leave her alone. Don't hurt her. Robert. Don't hurt her.

[*He throws* ROBERT *off her.* EVA *screams.* SKELLY, *seeing* NELLY, *looks up and runs toward her instinctively.*] Help her!

MARY [*to* NELLY, *from upstairs at the* Windrod *house*]. Nelly, Nelly, there's someone out back, honey, having a terrible fight; they came through the woods and started yelling all kinds of things.

NELLY. Where was you? I thought you was in bed.

MARY. You better go out and see, honey.

NELLY *takes up a shotgun, throwing open the door.*

NELLY. What's going on? Who's there?

As Eva *screams,* NELLY *levels the shotgun at* SKELLY'S *chest and fires first one, then the other, barrel.* SKELLY *falls, violently spun about by the force of the gun. In production it is important that the blanks for the shotgun be very loud, about half as much power as in actual shots; the powder from the gun smokes the entire stage until the end of the play. The* CONGREGATION *moves from their stationary position as* SKELLY *hits the floor. They mill a brief moment. The gun is passed, without much interest from one to the other of the men:* JUDGE, JOSH, PECK, *and the* TRUCKER. *The cast assembles at the court, blocking* SKELLY *from the audience's view.*

JUDGE [*immediately after the* CONGREGATION *begins to move*]. State your name.

ROBERT [*moving into the witness stand*]. Robert Conklin.

JUDGE. Do you swear to tell the whole truth and nothing but the truth, so help you God?

ROBERT. I do.

JUDGE. There's nothing to be nervous about, Robert. We want you to tell the court, just in your own words, what happened on the night in question. Can you do that?

ROBERT. Yes, I think.

JUDGE. We know this has been a terrible shock to you——

ROBERT. —I'm okay, I think. See—Eva and I were walking. We do quite frequently. Just wandering through the woods, talking. And we noticed that it had begun to get dark so we thought we had better start back—and we were heading back toward the main street, that would be west. And Eva thought she heard something behind us and we listened but we didn't hear it again so I assumed we were hearing things. Or it was our imagination. And it got dark pretty fast. And we were just coming into the clearing right behind the mill. Windrod's mill. And uh, we heard something again and this time we saw something behind the trees and we started running. More as a joke than anything—and then he started running too. And it was Skelly, and I wasn't afraid of him, but I knew he'd never liked my brother, and he started running too. He must have been following us all the time; everybody knows how he spies on people; I guess just as we broke into the clearing—and he came from nowhere. [*Crowd reaction.*] And he took us by surprise and he pushed me—he hit me from behind; I don't know if I passed out or not. [*Crowd murmur.*] He's immensely strong. [*Crowd murmur.*] And I heard a ringing in my ears and I saw what he was trying to do, and everything went white. And he pushed me.

EVA [*screams as loud as possible*]. AHHHHHHHHHHH! AHHH-HHHHHHHHHH! AHHHHHHHHHHHHH!

EVELYN. Oh, God, oh God, baby, my baby.

EVA. NO! no, no, no, no, no.

EVELYN. See her crippled body. See her broken back; why? Why has God cursed me with this burden? I don't complain, I ask why? We love Him. We bless Him. Praise Him.

Everyone freezes. Tableau. Silence.

PATSY [*off*]. You know I saw you the day you first came into town, I'll bet. I've seen you a lot. Up at the Hilltop. I told Lena I liked you. No, no, come on. Yes, it's all right; I want you to. You know I do.

WALTER [*off*]. I've got nothing with me.

PATSY [*off*]. I know, it doesn't matter. You wouldn't wash your feet with your socks on. Be easy. Did you know I'd watched you? Huh? Did you? Huh? Did you know I had?

WALTER [*off*]. No. I've seen you a couple of times.

PATSY [*off*]. I told Lena I liked you. I don't like any of the boys here; they're terrible, shiftless; oh, they're all right. But nobody wants to spend their life here; not here in this place rotting away. Walter! You're name's Walter, isn't it? I found out. Oh. Oh, I love you, Walter. I do. I really do. I love you. Oh, I do. Really. Did you know that? I have since I saw you that first time. I do. I really do. I love you so much. I love you, oh, I do, I love you. I do. Oh, I love you, Walter. You're the only one I love; I do. Really, I do.

Pause. Silence. The people mill gently, leave the stage slowly, silently, a few at a time. SKELLY *lies on stage where he fell.*

Curtain.

DAYS AHEAD

A Monologue

Days Ahead was first presented by Joseph Cino at the Caffe Cino in New York City as half of a double bill with the author's *Sex Is Between Two People* on December 28, 1965. It was acted and directed by Neil Flanagan; lighting was by John P. Dodd.

DAYS AHEAD

A room. If furnished, furnished Victorian, with globe lamps and fringed table covers. One wall has obviously been built to divide the room in half; we cannot see what is on the other side of the wall. The visible half of the room should look as if it has been closed off for a long time, dusty, stale. A chair is the only real essential.

A man hurriedly enters. It is difficult to say how old he is. He has the look of a small businessman; you could guess he manages an antique shop or clock shop or occupies a routine position in some strongly established business—bookkeeper, etc. He enters as though he has walked up several flights of stairs. He looks excited, expectant, and almost joyous. He is perhaps forty-five, with that indefinite look of the permanently middle-aged; he might be sixty. He is not senile, in any case, but is quite fastidious. He walks to the wall as soon as he enters, raps several times, as if it were a routine. He is quite happy with himself.

My dear?

He raps on the wall again, as before.

Love?

Calling to the other side. Almost embarrassed, as a child.

I'm back; here I am. I know, you're thinking I've made a mistake and come a full day early; you're thinking, why, this is the thirteenth and not the fourteenth at all and, of course, you're right; I'm early, but I've made no mistake.

Very pleased with himself.

Can you guess? Well, here I am, standing here breathless, like a damn fool from all those stairs and so anxious I've not even sat down. When something marvelous occurs, I've always been like that. A day early, more or less, routine be hanged. Of course, who knows better than you; and it is marvelous! Can you guess? Can you tell I'm happy? But before, even before you knew me, as a student, away alone—never could wait. Christmastime, those times when I didn't go home and presents from uncles and aunts and all the family arrived, such excitement, with my studies piled up—still I couldn't wait. Never could. Christmas morning seemed so far away and what matter, because certainly they would

65

never know, and what matter—so invariably—with all the gifts, wrapped so brightly as they were—invariably the curiosity always —always got . . .

He has become quite winded, pauses now and takes a deep breath.

Oh, really. I must sit down. Let me pull up the chair—those stairs, I'm afraid . . .

He goes to the chair, brushes some dust off.

Oh, my.

Coughs slightly, still preoccupied with his thoughts, and begins to drag the chair to the wall.

Invariably the curiosity . . .

He coughs a little, finishes dragging the chair to the wall, and sits in it. He is not facing the wall, but the chair is situated alongside the wall, very close; his face should not be more than a foot from the wall. Sitting.

There. Oh, my. And it seems more dusty than ever.

Back to a kind of contented rapture.

Oh, my dear, my dear.

Adjusting himself in the chair.

Yes, that's more like it. Now. I know you're anxious for news, love, so I'll tell you that first.

Taking a very small note pad out of his pocket, the kind where the leaves fold over the top.

But when you hear the revelation—and it is a revelation—why, you'll say, or rather you'll think—well, why didn't he tell me first off—why, hang the news, that's the best news I could have heard is what you'll say.

Looking at the first page of the notebook.

Well, let's see. There isn't all that much. It seems I'm always thinking nothing important happens; and then I get on to myself for being so pessimistic and say, what exactly *has* happened? Write it down! Beth will want to know; you know how she cares about all those little things you think so trivial. And I press, I do—I press my mind for details that would be interesting, diverting, informative. And more often than not I have to conclude that as we grow older things that happen, things we would have found quite diverting, even scandalous some of them—well, not scandalous, eye-opening—seem—unimportant really. Ultimately—trivial.

Light pause. He wanders some from the point from time to time, but all in the nature of being helpful.

That's why it's so difficult to find something worthwhile, as we grow older.

Consulting his book.

The first month, a whole month—March—nothing.

He turns the blank page.

April, nothing.

Turns the page.

May, one note which seems now not as important as then.

Wandering slightly.

As usual April was the windy month—came in like a lion—May the wet one, June the balmy beginning of spring: the first sweetness. "May showers bring June flowers." Perhaps the other axiom pertains to some lower latitude, farther south. Or perhaps climatic conditions have actually altered; that could be possible.

Looking back at the book.

The note for May is a gathering. Mrs. Fields. A small party, rather the same crowd. You'll remember three years ago I mentioned the Fields had done their living room over in rust. Rust everywhere. Sepia, she called it. Looked like rust; rust everywhere. Well, they have lately changed from rust to milky-green. Milky-green everywhere. Can you picture it? It makes one quite long for the rust back again. And that was May.

Turning the page.

In June I went walking; I left work early one afternoon and went into the park. The jonquils were gone, but there were flowering trees everywhere. A rain had come the night before, a soft rain, and every flowering tree had a perfectly circular, white . . .

The word escapes him and he continues as if he had said it.

. . . that was quite lovely. But as rain will, it had also washed away the scent altogether. The flowers smelled of rain; nothing more. I remembered there, when we walked in the park, or I tried to. I couldn't place it exactly—the park has changed in the years since. I thought, in the autumn the trees will be bearing fruit—sweet—and no one will be there to eat it. It'll rot there on the ground, in the leaves. It's a very sad waste, a useful tree in an arboretum.

Turning a page for each month.

July, August, September: no autumn again this year. One day the leaves are green and the next they're dead. Brown. Fallen.

Turns the page.

October. Well, news indeed! It isn't important.

He puts the book away. Perhaps he has taken out a pair of gold-rimmed glasses to read the book, which he also puts away as he continues.

Let me tell you. I've brought with me a fork. I looked around for something stronger; I couldn't find a thing. It seems you're always with me lately.

The love and expectancy return to his face, to his voice.

I think about you so often. It was lovely once. Of course we knew that. And I've always said that when I began to feel restless, discontent, it was my fault; I've always freely admitted that. It was some deficiency in me. I admit it. I admitted it then, didn't I? Twenty years ago. Haven't I every year? I don't know; it's so easy to say you've always known something, always said something, when you've felt it and not had the courage to speak. But I'm sure, fairly certain, I said it. Even then. Some deficiency in me. And you know as well as I what that can lead to. Doubting, mistrust, and I wouldn't have it! It would have led to arguments which you know I could not have withstood. Bickering, petty arguments over nothing, magnified grotesquely. I've seen no beneficial qualities in quarreling. Perhaps that was the lack. Who am I to say? But I felt you would have grown discontent.

His hand passes over the wall.

And this impromptu wall. I promised to keep you informed, and I have!

Defensively.

But each year, when I talk to you, I scratch the wall: it's almost as if unconsciously I wanted to see you again, isn't it? I've never mentioned it, but I rub the wall with my hand, fill my fingernail with plaster, all white; dig and chip. . . . Whatever it was in me that——

Excited.

Do you sense what I'm saying? Do you know already? I looked for something other than a fork, but it's all that's around. Whatever it was—that deficiency, I feel—I've outlived. I think if a restlessness still exists, I'm willing to chance it anyway. Do you know?

He removes a fork from his pocket, and begins to dig, gently, unconsciously at the wall—just little jabs while he talks.

It's been so long that I couldn't be sure. But lately, this year, more each day, I've been able to feel it. Memories are sweeter even than ever; you seem so much dearer to me every day.

Digs.

It's been long and I've been foolish—I know people would say that. That I've been foolish to ever expect to regain that first awakening love, that first sweet efflorescence. But it isn't memories! This year more and more, for the first time, I begin to see, more each day, how I want you now. How I look forward to days ahead, with your love. And that's what I was never able to do. Only doubts, misgivings that, if I'd have let them grow, would have destroyed us. But I saw that and said, no, no, we had a perfect love: if you're losing your trust, recognize it and don't let it happen. Do something. If you can no longer think about the future, and you once dreamed of everlasting love, don't give up the dream, find it again.

He is digging at the wall, gently, regularly now.

And I've—I've—— Oh, God, do you know? That's why I couldn't wait; I had to come today, finally; as I said I would, and I've come back to you. I know maybe I was wrong to leave you alone. I've had to realize now that you might be—— My dear, I didn't know what I was doing. I was passionate. I was losing the thing most precious to me; but I must have been right. You see now? Because I've come back. The doubts have waned and I love you. I've—I've had to realize now that you might be ill without my care—or you could have grown to hate me; even though I've kept my word. Everything that might interest you I set down day by day to tell you. Still I know you could reject me now. If you do, I'll understand it now. I've lived a lonely struggle on my way back to you; if you no longer love me, I'll let you go. Walk away free. That's the chance I have to be willing to take, dear, and I am now. I promise you. I've been alone these years, I can live without happiness if you wouldn't be happy with me. But if you can. If you can! We'll be always together.

He pauses in the digging for a moment.

I was not about to stand on the shore and watch you sail away with a widening breach coming between us. I would never have done that.

He begins, more slowly.

But you've come to realize that. Haven't you? Oh, love, love. We can be happy again together now.

Continuing to dig at the plaster wall.

We'll walk in the park! Through the walks in the arboretum—if you'll have me back. We'll walk by the river in the summer and crowd under the cool, sweating viaduct during a rain, and I'll buy you a little globe paperweight with a toy snowstorm like you told me you had as a child. Do you remember? And then, if you forgive me, we'll go to parties and dance in the street and you can take me to where you grew up as a young girl and we'll cry over the ugly apartment buildings that's taken over the wooded lots and hills where you played—again. All over again—if you'll accept me— and I'll never doubt now that I'm sure, and I am sure. If you only are, and if you are, we'll be so happy, love.

A pause.

Can you hear it giving away, the wall?

The lights begin to dim, as he continues.

We'll walk in the park.

As the lights dim, his voice becomes softer and softer until he is no longer audible.

Through the walks in the arboretum. We'll walk by the river in the summer and crowd under the viaduct for privacy; and I'll buy you a little globe paperweight with a toy snowstorm, like you told me you had as a child. Do you remember . . . ?

The lights are gone.

THE MADNESS OF LADY BRIGHT

A Play in One Act

For
Neil Flanagan

CHARACTERS

LESLIE BRIGHT, *a man of about forty; he is a screaming preening queen, rapidly losing a long-kept "beauty"*

BOY ⎫ *both are very attractive, perhaps twenty-five, dressed in dark,*
GIRL ⎭ *simple, casual clothes*

The Madness of Lady Bright was first presented by Joseph Cino at the Caffe Cino on May 19, 1964. It was directed by Denis Deegan with sets by Joseph Davies, lighting by John Torrey, and had the following cast:

LESLIE BRIGHT	Neil Flanagan
GIRL	Carolina Lobravico
BOY	Eddie Kenmore

The production was revised with new casts and a redirection by William Archibald to run a total of 168 performances at the Cino.

THE MADNESS OF LADY BRIGHT

The stage within a stage is set as LESLIE BRIGHT's *one-room apartment. The walls are light and covered over with hundreds of signatures, or autographs, mostly only names, in every conceivable size and writing medium. The name "Adam" is prominent on one wall; on another is "Michael Delaney." There is a dresser with nail polish, hair brush, lipstick, various clutter across the top. A desk, chair, papers, telephone. A portable phonograph that works passably well and records. The room seems tucked like a pressing book with mementos, post cards, letters, photographs, pictures of men from body-building magazines. A bed with pink and white silk sheets is against one wall. A window looks out to the back of buildings across the back yard below, a scene like the seventies between Amsterdam and Columbus avenues in upper Manhattan. The room is very sunny. A hot, still summer afternoon.*

The characters of the BOY *and* GIRL *are used to move the action—to* LESLIE's *memories, moods. They express, as actors, various people, voices, lovers. Sometimes they should be involved, sometimes almost bored, impatient, sometimes openly hostile, as the people he has known.*

At curtain the three walk on and assume their positions. The BOY *and* GIRL *sit to the side, or either side;* LESLIE, *entering, carrying a telephone, in character, sits at the desk and dials a number. After a moment of half-listening, a doubletake, he turns to the couple.*

LESLIE [*broadly*]. Do you know what is comforting the world on Dial-A-Prayer this abysmally hot Saturday afternoon?

GIRL [*prefatorily, to the audience*]. Abysmally Hot Saturday Afternoon . . .

LESLIE [*cutting in, superior*]. You think lately perhaps you've been overly preoccupied with sex; you should turn to deeper, more solemn matters, and Dial-A-Prayer gives you: "The Lord is my Shepherd, I shall not want. He maketh me to *lie down* in green pastures." God, what an image. Out in a green pasture, yet. Well, Adam, if that isn't heaven. . . . Why didn't you maketh me to lie down in green pastures, Adam? Why didn't you just

75

maketh me to lie down? Why didn't you maketh me? [*He has been looking through an address book.*] Well, who would be home? [*Dials.*] Stalwart queen, I can't believe even you would walk the street in this heat. [*Hanging up.*] One day you're going to melt into the sidewalk [*Looking through the book*] into this little puddle of greasy rouge and nylons. [*Dials.*] Ring. Ring. [*Holds telephone receiver between his shoulder and ear, picks up the bottle of nail polish and polishes one nail.*] Ring. [*Looking at the hand.*] Ten rings, dear, that's enough for any girl. One for every finger. Cheap damn Chinese red. Junk. No one. No one is home. [*Waving hand to dry.*] That's ten, sweetheart—okay, one extra for the index finger—eleven, that's all, sorry. [*Hangs up sloppily.*] So, no one is home.

BOY. You're home.

LESLIE [*cutting in*]. *I'm* home, of course. Home. [*Looks around.*] Oh, god! Well, face it, girl; you'll drive yourself stir if you can't find someone else to drive. . . . [*He fans through the address book.*] Oh, to hell with you. [*Tossing it aside.*] You bore me. [*Affected voice.*] You bore me! [*Rather seriously.*] You are a pile of paper addresses and memories, paper phone numbers and memories, and you mean nothing to me. [*Trying to catch the line just said.*] You—I am surrounded—I am left with [*Rather desperately trying to catch the right phrasing of the line to write it down*] a—with paper memories and addresses. . . .[*Finds a piece of paper at the desk. With a pencil, bent over the desk.*] I am— how?

BOY. I am left with a—with paper memories.

GIRL. With paper addresses.

BOY. You are a pile of addresses and remembrances.

LESLIE. How did it go?

GIRL [*singing*]. "Memories, memories . . ."

LESLIE. How did it go?

BOY. I am a paper.

LESLIE. Oh, to hell with it. I should go out. [*Looking at the polished nail.*] If nothing else in the world, I am certain that that is the wrong color for me. [*Sitting down.*] I—I—— [*Totally different thought.*] I should never wear anything other than blue. Aqua. The color of the sea. [*Rising.*] I am Venus, rising from . . . and matching eye shadow. And nothing else. [*He looks in the mirror for the first time. Stops. Looks bitchily at his reflection.*] You. Are a faggot. There is no question about it any more—you are definitely a faggot. You're funny but you're a faggot. [*Pause.*] You have *been* a faggot since you were four years old. Three years old. [*Checking the mirror again.*] You're not *built* like a faggot— necessarily. You're built like a disaster. But, whatever your dreams, there is just no possibility whatever of your ever becoming, say, a lumberjack. You know? [*He has risen and is wandering aimlessly about the room.*]

GIRL. You know?

Music, very softly from outside.

LESLIE. I know. I just said it. None whatever. Oh, you're spinning around in your stupid room like Loretta Young for Christsake. You should have a long circular skirt and . . . [*Long stretching motion with his arm as he turns, imitating Loretta Young's television entrance.*] "Hello. John?" [*He stops. They all hear the music now, a Mozart concerto, very faint.*] Why, how lovely.

GIRL. How soft, distant. Isn't that lovely?

BOY. It is.

The three drift toward the window.

LESLIE. It must be coming from someone's apartment. Some faggot's apartment. [*They are at the window.*] He's turned on the Bach— no, it's Mozart. And he's preparing dinner nervously, with some simple salad and some complex beef stew. And they'll dine by candlelight and ruin their eyes. Sometimes in summer it seems the only way to remain sane is listening to the radios playing in the neighborhood. I haven't a radio myself; I discovered I was talking back to it so I kicked it out. I have only the phonograph you saw and some worn-out records.

The BOY and GIRL have become visitors.

GIRL. The music is lovely.

BOY. Where's it coming from, can you tell?

LESLIE. I don't know. Somewhere. It's nice at a distance like that. Sometimes in summer it seems the only way to remain sane is by listening to—of course, it's a mixed neighborhood. Oh, well. I get

Spanish guitars and a good deal of Flamenco music as well. Of course I enjoy that too. At a distance like that.

GIRL. So soft, like that.

BOY. It's all right.

They turn from the window.

LESLIE. Mozart has always been one of my favorites; I know, you'll say how ordinary, but Mozart and Bach, I believe they have—oh, I don't know. It's so immature to try to analyze music.

The window has become the doorway to a symphony hall; they exit, moving away slowly, and LESLIE lights a cigarette, as at intermission.

BOY. It isn't necessary to talk about it; you just listen to it.

LESLIE. Exactly. I know. But they'll intellectualize and say that *this* is like a sunset and *that*—I mean it's so phony.

GIRL. It is.

LESLIE. I get really passionately upset by that sort of thing. Music is not like a sunrise, it's like [*They are laughing at his joke before it is finished*] music, isn't it? I mean, isn't it?

GIRL. That's so true.

BOY. That's true.

They walk away. LESLIE remains standing in the same position. The music has faded away.

LESLIE [*continuing*]. I go to these concerts only to listen to the music, not to see the white cliffs of wherever-it-is. I only . . . [*Listens.*] It's stopped. [*Goes to window again.*] Why do you always hear that stupid concerto, the same one? There is no one out there who would have been playing it, is there? [*To the walls.*] Is there, Autographs? [*Listens.*] What was that? [*This is bawdy— Judy Garland yelling to her doting audience.*] What was that once more? [*Big.*] We'll stay all night and sing 'em all! [*A bow. Drops his cigarette.*] God damn! Burn the place down.

BOY [*correcting; this exchange rapidly, with almost sadistic inanity*]. Up.

GIRL. Burn the place *up.*

LESLIE. Up or down?

GIRL. Up or down.

BOY [*echo*]. Up or down?

LESLIE. Down or up? [LESLIE *sits at dresser.*]

GIRL [*cutting in*]. You're so damn sloppy; if you've got to smoke . . .

LESLIE [*cutting in*]. I don't *have* to smoke, I *prefer* to smoke.

GIRL [*cutting in*]. Got to smoke you could at least take a few elementary precautions not to burn the place down.

BOY. Up.

GIRL. Not to burn the place up.

LESLIE [*cutting in*]. I am a very nervous person and I have to have something to do with my hands and I *prefer* to smoke, if you don't mind! If you don't *Mind!*

GIRL. Well, you can buy your own cigarettes; don't expect me to supply cigarettes for you, and don't think I don't notice when you steal mine.

LESLIE. I wouldn't touch yours. . . .

GIRL. You can march down to the store and buy your own—if you're not ashamed to be seen there.

The BOY *has laughed chidingly at "march."*

LESLIE. Why would I be . . . [*Breaks off, turns to mirror.*] Hmm. [*Hands to sides of eyes, testily.*] Oh, not good. Not good at all. All those spidery little wrinkles showing your *a-g-e.* Exposing yourself, aren't you? And a gray hair or two—and your whole face just collapsing. Built like a disaster. [*Turning mirror away.*] Oh, do go away. [*To the back of mirror.*] You should be preserved somewhere. You are a very rare specimen that should be saved for posterity. *Lowered* into the La Brea tar pits in a time capsule as a little piece of the twentieth century that didn't quite come off. Along with an Olivetti typewriter and a can of—cream of celery soup. [*Turning mirror back again.*] Whatever you're telling me I don't want to hear it. I've heard it before from every bitchy queen alive. The old fey mare ain't what she used to be. But she's well preserved, you've got to give her that. A *line or two,* but holding together. By a thread. [*Rising.*] But she can sing like a nightingale. Well, nearly. And dance like Giselle. Giselle was a little willie— a willie is a fairy who dances in the woods. [*Almost as though telling a story to the* BOY *and* GIRL.] And, well, they tried to make Giselle's husband dance all night and she danced all night in his place. [*Aside.*] Didn't you, Giselle? You did. You saved his **life.**

[*To the walls.*] Now, what have I done for you? All my visitors—all the men who have visited this stupid apartment for the last ten or so years—what have I ever done for you? Well, let's face it, what did you ever do for me? Look at it that way. Precious little. [*Jumping onto the bed, tapping a finger against a crossed-out name.*] Oh, you! Quentin! I scratched your name off over a year ago; you gave me—what particular social disease was it you gave me? You with your neat little signature. Tight, like-a-spring-little-signature. You can always tell a man by the way he signs his name, and a tight signature is very, very bad, Quentin.

BOY. How come?

LESLIE [*walking away. Only mildly scolding*]. I have studied graphology and believe me, it is very, very *bad*, Quentin. You will undoubtedly give me some dreadful social disease. And you, another meek little signature. In pencil. But you were only an edge bashful, only shy. For a meek little signature, Arnold Chrysler, you weren't really bad. You were not Adam, but there was only one. You were none of you like—anything like—Adam. Well, Michael Delaney was wonderful indeed; marvelous indeed, but he was not Adam. [*Cheek to Adam's name.*] You were everything. You are what I remember. Always the dreams are you. [*Turning away, laughing.*] Dreams? Oh, my dear. Fantasies. Oh, you are definitely cracking. [*Into mirror.*] Mirror, you are—I am sorry to report—cracking up. [*Frustrated.*] I am losing my mind. I am. I am losing my faggot mind. I'm going insane. [*The Mozart returns, but never important —very distantly, and only for a few bars.*] It's this stupid apartment and the goddamned heat and *no one ever being at home!* [*To telephone.*] Why don't you answer? [*To himself.*] You are growing old and fat and insane and senile and old. [*Goes to phone, dials. Ends the nervous note, says with the phone:*] "The Lord is my"—yes, we know all that. [*Hangs up. Dials.*] All of you are never, ever, ever at home. [*Looking about the room as the phone rings on and on.*] You at least never had homes. You never lived in one place more than a week. Bums and vagabonds, all of you; even Adam, admit it. Tramp around the world, hustling your box from Bermuda to Bangkok! From Burma to Birmingham. How was Birmingham, Adam? What? Oh, don't lie to me, *everyone* has hustled his box in Birmingham. [*Notices the phone is in his hand, hangs up.*] Never home. At least you can

count on Dial-A-Prayer being home. [*Tosses book on the desk.*]
You, you whores, tramp-the-street bitches. Dial-A-Prayer, and
weather and the correct time and Pan American Airways travel
information and TWA and American and Delta and Ozark—and
the public library. You can count on—but an acquaintance? Don't
count on it. There is no one outside. [*Laughs.*] Well! [*To the* BOY
and GIRL.] A little action, huh? [*They laugh, party-like.*] I hate
beer, just a coke, please: Yes, I know they're both fattening, you
whore, I don't have to worry about that *yet!* Beauty isn't everything! . . . But then what is? Come on.

GIRL. Come on.

A rock and roll record comes up.

BOY. Come on. Let's dance.

LESLIE. Let's dance. [GIRL *dances with* BOY, LESLIE *dances with
imaginary partner. The* BOY *talks both for himself and* LESLIE's
partner. But LESLIE *doesn't know the dance.*] What is it? What
on earth? Oh, God, I couldn't do that. Zat new? Huh? Well tell
me the steps anyway.

BOY. Zeasy.

LESLIE. Walk through it once.

BOY. Just follow.

LESLIE. I'll try. Oh, God. [*Catching on, but not completely getting
it.*]

BOY. Zit.

LESLIE. Is it?

*They continue to dance, very fast, very tiring, until the end of the
record and it goes off. General noise.*

GIRL. Swell.

BOY. Thanks.

They walk away.

GIRL. Wheeh! It's so warm.

BOY. Yeah.

LESLIE. Is that all? Hell, it's over; put another quarter in. Ha! [*Comes
out of it.*] Goddamn. Every time, all over sweat. You crazy loon.
Stupid bitch. You should get dressed up and go down to the
beach, it's so damn muggy and hot they must need a little some-

thing to liven up the beach about now. [*Makes a quick single enormous cabbage rose of the top sheet and puts it on his head as a fashionable hat—walks across the room as in a beauty contest, singing low:*] "There she is, Miss America. . . ." [*Takes rose from head, holds it to cover himself—a vision of total nudity, raises his eyes to the imaginary judge's bench. With sunny brightness.*] Good morning, Judge! [*Pause.*] Your Honor. [*Tosses it aside, goes to dresser.*] Oh, dear. [*Pause.*]

BOY *and* GIRL *have been ignoring him.*

BOY [*to the actress quietly, privately*]. Did you go somewhere?

LESLIE [*tossing the sheet back to the bed*]. No.

GIRL. When?

BOY. Last night. Did you go out for a while?

GIRL. Oh, yes. I went for cigarettes.

BOY. I missed you. I rolled over for a second and stretched, you know —and you weren't there—and I thought where the hell—then I must have drifted off again. Got up and got dressed?

GIRL. I went out for a few minutes down to the drug store.

BOY. I wondered.

GIRL. It was raining.

BOY [*faking a hurt voice*]. Well, you might consider—I looked over expecting you to be there—and there was nothing but loneliness.

LESLIE [*to himself—listening in spite of himself*]. Loneliness. [*He is not looking toward them.*]

GIRL. You were asleep when I came back.

BOY. It's a terrible thing to wake up to loneliness. [LESLIE *looks sharply toward him at the word repeated.*]

GIRL. I came right back; it was wet as hell. You know?

LESLIE. You know nothing about loneliness. [*Long pause.*] I should go out. [*Seeing name on the wall.*] I should go out and look for you. . . . [*Creeping up on the name.*] Mich-ael De-lan-ey— [*Grabbing the wall.*] Gotcha! [*Turning from the wall.*] Good Lord—eight years ago—you would be how old by now? Oh well, old hustlers never die, they just start buying it back! [*Turning back to the wall.*] You were very good, I remember that. And who else? [*Going over the names.*] So-so; fair; clumsy, but cute anyway; too intelligent; Larry; good, I remember; A minus, and that's very good; undersized; very nice; *oversized*, but I'm not complaining. [*Suddenly angry.*] Samuel Fitch! [*Runs to the desk for a pencil.*] Samuel Fitch! [*Scratches the name off.*] No, I thought you were gone! You bitch! You liar! You vicious faggot! You *Queer!* You were not a man, you were some worm. Some smelly worm. [*Feeling better.*] Of course, you couldn't help it, you were *born* a worm. Once a worm always a worm, I always say. [*Looking back at the erased name.*] Oh. Poor Samuel. You really couldn't help it, could you? You were queer but you couldn't help it. Domineering mother, probably. What was it—that was sweet—you said. You said my body was smooth. [*The Mozart is back, softly but getting louder.*] Hairless, that's what you liked about it. You said I moved well, too, didn't you? Well, *I do* move well. I move *exceptionally* well. [*Sits on the side of the bed. Giselle music is added to the Mozart, and in a moment the rock and roll also begins.*] And I haven't a hair on my body. I'm as hairless and smooth as a newborn babe. I shave, of course, my underarms; no woman would go around with hair under her arms. It's just not done. Lately. In America anyway. [*Stretches his legs.*] And my legs— they're smooth. They are. [*Feeling the backs of his legs.*] I have— I [*Nervously.*] I have varicose veins in my legs. I can't wear hose. I have hideous, dreadful legs. I have blue, purple, *black* veins in my legs. They give me pain—they make me limp, they ache, they're ugly. They used to be beautiful and they are bony and ugly. Old veins. [*The* BOY *and* GIRL *begin to rub their legs and arms and to moan low.*] Old legs, dancing legs; but the veins! They get tired. And when they get [*Fast*] old they get tired and when they get tired they get slow and when they get slow they get stiff and when they get stiff they get brittle and when they get brittle they break and the veins break and your bones snap and your skin sags. . . . The veins in my arms and legs—my veins are old and brittle and the arteries break—your temples explode your veins break like glass tubes—you can't walk you can't dance you can't speak; you stiffen with age. Age takes you over and buries you; it buries you under—under—*my veins,* my arms, my body, my heart, my old callused hands; my ugly hands; my face is collapsing. I'm losing my mind. [*The* BOY *finally screams a long, low, "Oh." The* GIRL *screams nervously, "I'm going insane."*] I'm going insane. I'm going insane!

BOY. My veins, my arteries.

The Boy *and* Girl *speak the next two lines simultaneously.*

Girl. I'm being buried.

Boy. I'm old; I'm growing old.

Girl [*singing*]. "Memories, memories."

The music has now reached its loudest point.

Leslie [*speaking over* Girl's *singing*]. I'm losing my *mind. I'm
losing my mind. Oh, God, I'm losing my mind!* [*He falls panting
onto the bed. The only music left is the Mozart, very far away.
After a moment he gets up. He notices his pants leg is pulled up;
he slowly pulls it down.*] I. . . .

Girl [*chattering madly*]. If you must smoke you could at least buy
your own.

Boy. How did it go, memories and paper and addresses on the walls
and . . . ?

Girl. And don't tell me . . .

Leslie [*sits on side of the bed. To himself*]. I should.

Girl. And don't tell me you don't snatch mine; I've seen you. I
sometimes count them, you know. Did you ever think about that?

Leslie. I—I should go out. [*Rises, walks to desk, sits.*] That way
insanity, Leslie. That way the funnyfarm, Lady Bright. The men
in white, Mary. And watch it, because you know you look like a
ghost in white. You have never, ever worn white well. [*Rising.*]
You should never be seen in any color other than pink. Candy
pink. Candy pink and white candy stripes. Silk.

Girl. Well, of course.

Leslie [*walking toward the window*]. Someone is playing their radio;
I wonder what station plays Mozart all day long. [*The* Boy *has
moved to beside the bed. He is buckling his belt.*] I know you
don't understand it, but I do. Your pants are on the chair.

Boy. Yeah, I found them. You're good, I'll say that.

Leslie [*pleased*]. Sometimes I just like to stand and listen to the
music from someone's radio. I've done that a lot this summer. I
live alone. [*He continues to look out the window, away from the*
Boy.]

Boy. I said you're good.

LESLIE. Well, of course. You see the names. Did you notice the names on the wall?

BOY [*seeing them*]. Yeah. I mean I see them now. You do it?

LESLIE. Of course not! They're autographs. No one has refused me. And I'll want yours, too, of course.

BOY. My what?

LESLIE. Your name, your autograph.

BOY. On the wall?

LESLIE. Yes. Whenever you want to write it. There's an ink pen on the table if you haven't one.

BOY [*finding it and going to the wall*]. Yeah. Okay, you got it.

LESLIE. Don't tell me where. Move away now. [*He turns.*] Now. [*Surveying the walls.*] There. Oh, so large, you egoist; it surely wasn't difficult to find it. Michael Delaney. You're Irish?

BOY. Yeah.

LESLIE. Irish. [*Distantly disappointed.*] Well, it isn't romantic, is it? It's not Russian or Sicilian or one of those, but I've got nothing against the Irish. Any more. You have raised my opinion of them, I'll admit, considerably. [*The* BOY *walks away, sits down.*] I thought you only drank a good deal, but I find you have a capacity for other things as well. And it's just as well to add a favorite nationality; I was guessing you as Jewish; you don't mind me saying that—the dark hair, you know—but with a name like Michael Delaney you couldn't be anything else. [*The music has faded slowly out.* LESLIE *looks out the window again.*] They've turned the radio down so I can't hear it now. I tell you, [*A quick glance at the name*] Michael, it's no fun. It's no fun living here in this stupid apartment by myself listening to my few records and the neighbor's radio; I should like someone, I think sometimes, [*Being delicate*] living here some times. Or maybe somehow not living here but coming here to see me often. Then I'd wash the walls—wash off everyone else. Wash them off and kiss them good-by—good riddance. I've even thought I wouldn't mind, you know, just letting someone live here, scot free; I could prepare the meals—and do things. I—want to *do* things for someone who could live here. And he could sleep here, every night. It's really lovely—or would be—with the music. I'd like something like that, it [*Turning*] gets so lonely here by . . . [*But of course, he's gone.* LESLIE *glances at the* BOY *sitting. To the* GIRL.] This dumb room. [*To the walls.*] Dumb! Mute! All you goddamned cobwebby corners, you stare down at me while I die of boredom; while I go insane because everyone I call is gone off somewhere. Once more. [*Goes to phone, dials, listens to the ringing.*] Once. Twice. Thrice. Quadrice. Screw. [*Limply he puts his finger on the cradle, clicking off. Raises it and dials from memory another number.*]

GIRL. Good afternoon, American Airlines. May we help you?

LESLIE. Yes. [*Pause.*] Fly me away from here. [*Clicks her off, leaving his finger on the phone. Long pause. Reflecting, bitchily.*] Oh, well, fly yourself, fairy; you've got the wings. All God's chil'un got wings, Leslie. That's your disastrous body: wings and ass.

BOY. You've got a nice body. You know, a young body. How old are you, about nineteen? [LESLIE *is surprised, almost stunned by the line. The* BOY *repeats the cue.*] How old are you, about nineteen? [*The* BOY *has entered the room.*]

LESLIE [*sadly; remembering*]. Twenty. [*The scene now is played with young, fresh buoyancy.*] And you're what? The same age about, aren't you?

BOY. Twenty-one. Get drunk legally, any state.

LESLIE. I've never—I'm almost embarrassed—I've never met any-one as—well, I'm never at a loss for words, believe me. I don't know what you have—anyone so good looking as you are. [BOY *laughs.*] What do you do? Are you a weight lifter?

BOY. Who—me? I don't do nothing. Bum around.

LESLIE. Bum around.

BOY. Been in every state.

LESLIE. Just bumming around?

BOY. One state pays for the next, you know?

LESLIE. You hustle, I guess. I mean—do you only hustle? I . . .

BOY [*cutting in*]. That's right. Oh, well, for kicks too; sometimes. Why not? When the mood hits me.

LESLIE. I wish to God it would hit you about now.

BOY. Yeah. Rough night, kid. Sorry.

LESLIE. Oh.

Boy [*looking around*]. Come on, they'll be other nights. I said I like you; you're a nice kid. We'll make it. I'll promise you.

Leslie. You will?

Boy. I'll promise you that.

Leslie. Good. Then I'll wait.

Boy. How long you been in this pad?

Leslie. About a month. Everything's new. I painted the walls myself.

Boy. You ever seen one of these?

Leslie. What? A grease pencil? Sure, I used to work in the china department of this stupid store; we marked dishes with them.

Boy. Mind if I do something?

Leslie. What am I supposed to say? [*Earnestly.*] No. I don't mind if you do something. Anything.

Boy. Something to remember me by. [*Goes to wall.*]

Leslie. What? *What?* Are you writing—your name? Hey, on my fresh wall? [*The* Boy *turns smilingly to him.*] What the hell, it looks good there.

Boy. Yeah. I'll see you around.

Leslie. Where are you going? [*No answer.* Leslie *is in the present now. The* Boy *walks to his chair and sits.*] Where are you going? Not you. Don't leave now. Don't. Adam. You're not leaving. Come back here, don't go away; you were the one I wanted. The only one I wanted, Adam! Don't go away! [*Wildly.*] Don't go, Adam; don't go, Adam.

Girl. Unrequited love is such a bore.

Boy. Sad.

Girl. Left him flat, didn't he?

Boy. The only one he wanted.

Leslie. Oh, God, that way, honey, is madness for sure. Think about Adam and you've had it, honey. Into the white coat with the wrap-around sleeves.

The following dialogue between the Boy *and* Girl *takes place simultaneously with* Leslie's *next speech.*

Girl. It's sad, really.

Boy. It is. It really is. The only one he wanted really was Adam.

GIRL. And he never had him.

BOY. Never saw him after that.

GIRL. Of course he would have gone mad either way, don't you think?

BOY. Oh, yes.

GIRL. Drove himself to it, I mean. He couldn't have possibly lived a sane life like that.

BOY. Some pansies live a sane life and some don't. Like anyone else, I suppose.

GIRL. Well, not exactly.

BOY. I mean some go nuts and some don't. Some just go insane.

GIRL. Mad.

BOY. Nuts.

GIRL. Lose their balance, you know.

LESLIE [over the above. Moves to the record player and goes through the records, finds one.] What I should have is some music. I'm so sick of music for companionship. But it's better than [Looks at the telephone] you queens! Never-at-home sick queens! [Puts a record on. It is Judy Garland, singing a fast, peppy number. The volume is kept very low.] Now that's better. That's a little better. I can dance to that one. [He dances, as with a partner, but he dances a slow, sexy number as the music continues fast.] There. I like the way you . . . Oh, you think I follow well. I'm glad you think I follow—I have a good sense of rhythm, I've always been told that I move well. I get lonely, but I've been told I move well. I sometimes just stare at the corners of my room, would you believe that, and pray [He stops dancing and stands still.] And pray for . . . [Stops, panting.] I want—I want . . . [But he can't say it.]

GIRL [with comic remove]. He wants to die, I believe.

BOY. I think that's what he's trying to say.

GIRL. Well, it's easy to understand; I mean you couldn't expect him to live like that.

BOY. He's effeminate.

GIRL. No one can want to live if they're like that.

BOY. It's all right on girls.

LESLIE. Why do you let me live if you know it?

GIRL [to BOY]. What could we do?

LESLIE. Why?

BOY. No one should live who's like that.

LESLIE. Giselle. Giselle, you saved him. You danced all night and you danced till dawn and you saved him. You did, you saved him; you danced for him. They let you save him.

GIRL. He used to be an intelligent fellow.

BOY. He was. He was a bright kid.

GIRL. Quick-thinking.

LESLIE. Why do you let me live if you know it? Can't you see I'm going insane alone in my room, in my hot lonely room? Can't you see I'm losing my mind? I don't want to be the way I am.

GIRL. He doesn't like the way he is.

BOY. He'd like to be different.

GIRL. He looks different enough to me.

BOY. Extraordinary, I'd say.

LESLIE. You could have killed me as a child, you could have.

GIRL. Christ! How can you play those goddamned records? Do you have to blare that *music? Do* you? *You dance around in your room all day.* Do something worth while why don't you?

LESLIE. You could have.

GIRL. Do something worth while.

LESLIE [as before to Michael Delaney]. I'd like to do something. [Suddenly.] No. We won't have this music. [He's wild now, excited.] We won't have this music. [Strip music comes in over the Garland.] We'll have a party. We'll have a show. I'll give you a show!

BOY. He's going to give you a show. I think.

GIRL. Turn that off!

LESLIE goes to music. He turns it by accident to full volume, gets nervous, scratches the needle all the way across the record, at full volume. It clicks off. The other music goes off too.

LESLIE [turning to them]. What would you like?

BOY [to GIRL]. What would you like?

GIRL [*to* LESLIE]. What would you like?

LESLIE [*happily*]. Oh, me! God. I—would—like . . . We won't have a show, we'll have a royal dance; a cotillion; a nice beautiful dance.

GIRL. A ball! Wonderful!

BOY. Lady Bright requests your presence . . .

LESLIE. A beautiful party. [*Grabs the sheet and winds it around himself.*]

BOY. May I have the pleasure?

GIRL. I hardly know what to say.

Mozart music comes up.

LESLIE. And I shall be the queen! I dance with the most grace. I will be selected queen by popular demand. I dance like a flower on the water. [*Mozart up. They dance around in a whirl.*] I dance like a flower. I shall dance with Adam and you shall dance with whom you please. No, I have no more room on my program, I am dreadfully sorry, young man . . . [*Still dancing.*] I am dancing tonight with only one man, you know what that means.

GIRL. She's so lovely.

BOY. She's so beautiful.

GIRL. Did you catch her name?

LESLIE. My name is Giselle! I am Giselle! [*Running to mirror.*] I'm the fairest at the ball. I am the loveliest. *I am young. I am young and lovely. Yes, I am young!* [*He bends over the dressing table and returns to the mirror. He takes up lipstick and smears it across his lips, half his face.*] I am young tonight. I will never be old. I have all my faculties tonight. [*The people have continued to dance.* LESLIE *returns and they whirl about. Other music joins the Mozart—Giselle, the rock and roll, the strip number.*] I am beautiful. I am happy! [LESLIE *falls down. They continue to dance about him. The music stops. Then comes on. Stops. Returns. A pulsating effect.*] Excuse me, I must have . . . [*Music continues loudly.*] My arms are so tired. My legs. I have bad legs; I don't walk too well. The veins in my legs are getting old, I guess. . . . [*This is light, chattery talk.*] I grow tired easily. *I grow brittle and I break. I'm losing my mind, you know. Everyone knows when they lose their mind. But I'm so lonely!* [*The music stops.* LESLIE *looks up. The* BOY *and* GIRL *exit to opposite sides. As if to a man standing over him.*] I'm sorry. I just slipped and . . . [*Turning to the other side. There is a "man" there, too.*] Oh, thank you. [*Allowing the man to help him up, still with the sheet as a gown; softly to the man, intimately.*] I'm sorry—I hate to trouble you, but I—I believe I've torn my gown. I seemed to have ripped . . . Oh, no, it can be repaired. Yes, I'm sure it can. But would you take me home now, please? [*There is a pause.*] Just take me home, please; take me home, please. Take me home now. Take me home. *Please take me home.* [*The music now comes on and builds in a few seconds to top volume.* LESLIE *screams above it. He drops the sheet; it falls down around him.*] TAKE ME HOME, SOMEONE! TAKE ME HOME! [*The music stops.* LESLIE *has run to the wall, to a far-off area, leaning against the wall. The Mozart is the only music remaining. Softly, whispering against the wall—to himself.*] Take me home. Take me home. Take me home. Take me home. Take me home. Take me home. Take me home. Take me home. Take me home. . . .

The lights fade out slowly.

Curtain.

WANDERING

A Turn

CHARACTERS

HE

SHE

HIM

HE, SHE, and HIM are all about twenty-five. The stage which can be very small, should have a bench to be used as chair, bed, couch, bench, whatever. HE and SHE are standing at attention, side by side. HIM enters and sits. The actors should retire to the "Attention" position when not speaking. Actions and props should be pantomimed, and the play should be done very rapidly, without pause except toward the end, as indicated. The play runs through HIM's life, recapping several times at the end. Actions and characterizations should be very simple.

Wandering was first presented by Joseph Cino at the Caffe Cino as part of the 1966 Easter Show on April 10, 1966, with Marshall W. Mason, Lanford Wilson, and Zita Litvinas in the cast directed by Marshall W. Mason.

WANDERING

SHE. Where have you been?

HIM. Wandering around.

SHE. Wandering around. I don't know why you can't be a man; you just wait till the Army gets a-hold of you, young man.

HE. They'll make a man of you——

SHE. Straighten you out.

HE. A little regimentation.

SHE. Regulation.

HE. Specification.

SHE. Indoctrination.

HE. Boredom.

SHE. You'll get up and go to bed.

HE. Drill; march.

SHE. Take orders.

HE. Fight.

SHE. Do what they tell you.

HE. Keep in step.

SHE. Do your part.

HE. Kill a man.

SHE. You'll be a better person to live with, believe me. As a matter of fact, your father and I are getting damned tired of having you around.

HE. Looking after you.

SHE. Making your bed.

HE. Keeping you out of trouble.

SHE. How old are you, anyway?

HIM. Sixteen.

HE. Sixteen—well, my God.

SHE. Shouldn't you be drafted before long?

HIM. Two years.

SHE. You just better toe the mark.

HE. How long at your present address?

HIM. Six months.

HE. Any previous experience as an apprentice?

HIM. No, sir.

HE. Where did you live before that?

HIM. I was just wandering around.

HE. Not good. Draft status?

HIM. Well, I haven't been called but——

HE. We like fighters on our team, fellow.

HIM. Well, actually I'm a conscientious——

SHE. Sit down. Roll up your sleeve. Take off your shirt. Stick out your tongue. Bend over, open your mouth, make a fist, read the top line. Cough. [HIM *coughs.*]

SHE. Very good.

HIM. Thank you.

SHE. Perfect specimen.

HIM. I do a considerable amount of walking.

HE. I don't follow you.

HIM. I don't believe in war.

HE. There's no danger of war. Our country is never an aggressor.

HIM. But armies, see—I don't believe in it.

HE. Do you love your country?

HIM. No more than any other, the ones I've seen.

HE. That's treason.

HIM. I'm sorry.

HE. Quite all right; we'll take you.

HIM. I won't go.

HE. Service is compulsory.

HIM. It's my right.

HE. You'll learn.

HIM. I don't believe in killing people.

HE. For freedom?

HIM. No.

HE. For love?

HIM. No.

HE. For money?

HIM. No.

HE. We'll teach you.

HIM. I know, but I won't.

HE. You'll learn.

HIM. I can't.

HE. You're going.

HIM. I'm not.

HE. You'll see.

HIM. I'm sure.

HE. You'll see.

HIM. I'm flat-footed.

HE. You'll do.

HIM. I'm queer.

HE. Get lost.

SHE. I'm lost.

HIM. I'm sorry.

SHE. Aren't you lost?

HIM. I wasn't going anyplace in particular.

SHE. That's unnatural.

HIM. I was just wandering.

SHE. What will become of you?

HIM. I hadn't thought of it.

SHE. You don't believe in anything.

HIM. But you see, I do.

HE. I see.

HIM. It's just that no one else seems to believe—not really.

HE. I see.

HIM. Like this pride in country.

HE. I see.

HIM. And this pride in blood.

HE. I see.

HIM. It just seems that pride is such a pointless thing; I can't believe in killing someone for it.

She. Oh, my God, honey, it isn't killing; it's merely nudging out of the way.

Him. But we don't need it.

She. Think of our position, think of me, think of the children.

Him. I am.

She. You're shiftless is what it is.

Him. I'm really quite happy; I don't know why.

She. Well, how do you think I feel?

Him. Not too well, really.

She. Where does it hurt?

He. Nothing to worry about.

She. Yes, sir.

Him. Thank you.

She. And that's all for the morning; Mr. Trader is on line six.

Him. Thank you; send Wheeler in.

He. How are you, old boy?

Him. Not well, I'm afraid.

She. Don't be; it isn't serious.

He. Just been working too hard.

She. Why don't you lie down.

He. Best thing for you.

She. I know, but he was quite handsome—a gentle man.

He. Bit of a radical though—not good for the family.

She. I know.

He. You're better off.

She. I have a life of my own.

He. . . . you have a life of your own.

She. He was such a lost lamb.

He. Never agreed with anyone.

She. Arguments everywhere we went.

He. What kind of disposition is that?

She. I don't know what I ever saw in him.

He. You need someone who knows his way around.

SHE. I do.

HE. I do.

Pause.

SHE. I don't know why you can't be a man.

HE. Keep in step.

SHE. Toe the mark.

HE. Draft status?

SHE. Stick out your tongue.

HE. You'll learn.

SHE. What'll become of you?

HE. I see.

SHE. Think of the children.

HE. Best thing for you.

SHE. I do.

Pause.

HE. I see.

HIM. I mean that can't be the way people want to spend their lives.

SHE. Trader on line six.

HIM. Thank you.

HE. Just been working too hard.

SHE. I do.

Pause.

SHE. Where?

HIM. Wandering.

HE. I see.

HIM. They'll believe anything anyone tells them.

HE. I see.

HIM. I mean that can't be the way people want to spend their lives.

SHE. That's all for the morning.

HIM. Quite happy.

HE. Best thing for you.

SHE. I do.

HE. I do.

Pause.

SHE. Where have you been?

Pause.

HIM. Can it?

THIS IS THE RILL SPEAKING

A Play for Voices in One Act

For
David Starkweather
in return for *You May Go Home Again*

CHARACTERS

(Grouped for each of six actors)

MOTHER / PEGGY

WILLY / ELLIS / EARL

JUDY / MARTHA

KEITH / TED / TOM / 2ND FARMER

ALLISON / MAYBELLE ROBINSON

MANNY / WALT ROBINSON / FATHER / 1ST FARMER

The action of the play takes place on and around an elevated porch with a white railing. There are steps and a number of chairs opposite the swing. Scenes should be played on the porch and steps, at both sides of the porch, and in front. Lighting should be the scattered light of sun through trees. The actors group and regroup, wandering about the set. The play is meant for six voices: three women and three men. All have moderately strong Ozark accents.

This Is the Rill Speaking was first presented by Joseph Cino at the Caffe Cino, New York City, on July 20, 1965, with the following cast:

MOTHER / PEGGY	Alice Conklin
WILLY / ELLIS / EARL	Michael Warren Powell
JUDY / MARTHA	Claris Erickson
KEITH / TED / TOM / 2ND FARMER	John Kramer
ALLISON / MAYBELLE	Jacque Lynn Colton
MANNY / WALT / FATHER / 1ST FARMER	George Harris

The play was directed by the author, lighting by Earl Eidman, stage manager Richard Camargo.

The play subsequently toured through Europe with La MaMa Repertory Company under the direction of Tom O'Horgan and opened as part of the *Six from La MaMa* program at the Martinique Theater in New York on April 11, 1966.

THIS IS THE RILL SPEAKING

Actions may be pantomimed, physical elements may or may not be used, i.e., there may or may not be a window, though the MOTHER *will appear to be looking out of one.*

MOTHER. Well, there goes Walt Robinson, up to the post office. Willy, do you want to run and stop him?

WILLY. Run and stop him? What for?

MOTHER. You could offer to go for him, it'd be a good thing.

WILLY [*cutting in*]. What do you mean? He'll stay around the post office all day. It's the only thing he does all day long.

MOTHER. I suppose.

JUDY. Besides, who could be heard with him?

MOTHER. You shouldn't say that, Judy.

WILLY. He knows he's hard of hearing.

JUDY. Hard? He's never heard a word I've said to him, I don't think, and I yell my lungs out.

MOTHER. Well, you'd think they'd move a little closer to the square so he wouldn't have that hill to climb.

WILLY. It's the only thing he does.

MOTHER. I know.

JUDY. He doesn't even know what my *voice* sounds like, and I scream my lungs out to him.

MOTHER. Maybelle Robinson is over on her porch there.

WILLY. That's all she does. She spends her whole life there.

MOTHER. I suppose I should go over and keep her company.

JUDY. Why don't you talk to somebody younger? You're always talking to her. She never says anything worth hearing.

WILLY. I'm gonna go down by the river.

MOTHER. I don't know what to have for supper.

WILLY. They're tearing down that old bridge.

MOTHER. What old bridge is that?

103

WILLY. That old bridge by the fork.

MOTHER. There's no bridge there. You mean those rocks?

WILLY. It used to be a railroad bridge, years ago.

MOTHER. Who told you that?

WILLY. I don't know.

JUDY. Peggy should be coming over.

MOTHER. Peggy Harper is not coming over here.

JUDY. I told you.

MOTHER. I wish you wouldn't spend so much time with that girl.

JUDY. Peggy Harper is the nicest girl in the junior class.

MOTHER. That's not what I've been hearing.

JUDY. Well, I can't help it if you've been listening to Maybelle Robinson. I don't know what she has against Peggy.

MOTHER. She runs around half naked, and her fat as a tub. I'd think that girl would lose some weight or cover herself, one.

JUDY. Peggy is my friend and she can't help it if she has gland trouble.

MOTHER. Well, she could cover her bare legs; she looks like two sides of ham.

WILLY. She just eats too much.

JUDY. Well, she has gland problems.

MOTHER. Don't you leave the house in that halter and shorts either.

JUDY. What's wrong with a halter? It's more than a bathing suit.

MOTHER. I'm not going to have you talked about all over town.

WILLY. I'm going down to the river.

MOTHER. You stay away from the bridge if they're working down there. We don't need you knocked in the river and drowned.

WILLY. They're using the rocks to build a house, way up on the hill.

MOTHER. Young lady, don't you leave this house dressed like that.

JUDY. Peggy's coming over and we're only going to sit out on the back steps and talk.

MOTHER. Well, don't you leave your yard. Dressed like that.

JUDY. I'm not going to.

MOTHER. Willy, do you think your dad would mind if we had liver?

WILLY. We had liver last night.

MOTHER. We haven't had liver in a week. I don't think your dad likes liver really.

MAYBELLE. It looks like it's gonna *do* something.

MOTHER. Probably not till evening.

MAYBELLE [*curious; mysteriously; peering down the road*]. What's that a-coming up the street? Is that that junk man? I wonder what he thinks he's a-doing? What's he a-doing? Now he's stopped. Looks like something was about to fall off his cart. He's tying it *on* or *some*thing. Yes, it's gonna do something before long. You know Rachel Jackson had a girl.

MOTHER. When did she? Rachel Jackson a baby girl?

MAYBELLE. Yesterday afternoon and her over forty. Nobody even knew she was carrying it, fat as she is. You couldn't tell. And she didn't see fit to let a body know.

MOTHER. A baby girl. Where is she now?

MAYBELLE. Up to the hospital. Baby's in an incubator. Tiny thing. Born a month early from what I hear. Blue as a turnip. They had to give it blood. Her mother ought to know better than to have a child at her age and as fat as she is. Little thing weighed five pounds even.

MOTHER. Rachel Jackson with a new baby girl and her with two boys out of school nearly.

MAYBELLE. It'll die.

MOTHER. Oh, you shouldn't say that. Five pounds isn't that bad. [*She "tuts" some.*]

MAYBELLE. Poor little thing. [*She "tuts."*] Blue as a turnip.

MOTHER. It'll be all right.

MAYBELLE. It doesn't have a chance from what I hear. It'll break that poor woman's heart.

MOTHER. It would that for sure.

MAYBELLE. Serves her right, fat as she is.

MOTHER. It'll probably rain by evening. Cool things off some. Today's gonna be a scorcher.

MAYBELLE. There he goes again. I guess he got that tied on. Whatever it was. Turning down toward Mrs. Stut's. Now, what business do you suppose he has down that way? Walt's hearing is getting worse; I swear I think it is.

MOTHER. I saw him heading up toward town.

MAYBELLE. I suppose he'll be up there all day long. That's all he does. Stands around with all those old men up there. Grunting around. Laughing. I don't know what he's laughing about, he can't hear a thing they're saying. I don't know what good it does him. He didn't hear the alarm this morning. Can't eat a thing but mashed potatoes.

MOTHER. I know.

MAYBELLE. Mashed potatoes and milk and some cully-flower. They took him off salt.

TOM [young—fourteen; rapid exchange here]. You hear about Ben?

WILLY. Yeah, I heard they called off his party. He didn't come to school.

TOM. His mom wouldn't let him have it. You know why?

WILLY. Mr. Hawkins said he got sick.

TOM. He got sick all right. He was home. You know why—his mom *caught* him.

WILLY. When did she?

TOM. Yesterday noon. He come home for lunch and was in his room and she came in without knocking.

WILLY. What'd she do? He should've locked the door.

TOM. She beat the tar outta him. He said he almost cried. And made him swear on the Bible that he wouldn't ever do it again.

WILLY. What did she do that for?

TOM. She said he'd go blind and go crazy and go to hell.

WILLY. That's a lot of baloney. You think he'll quit?

TOM. He said he had to: she pressed his hand right against the Bible and made him swear.

WILLY. What a mean thing to do. She wouldn't let him have his birthday party, I know that for sure—he didn't come back to school and Old Man Hawkins came in our class and said the party was called off 'cause Ben was sick.

TOM. He was sick all right. His mom's gonna make him go to work this summer. He said he didn't mind, he wanted to anyway.

WILLY. Boy, that'd be terrible to have your mom walk right in on you. He used to do it three or four times a day. Every day at recess I know.

Том. Well, he won't any more.

Judy. I wish they'd be a breeze and cool things off some.

Willy. That'll teach him.

Judy. Some anyway.

Willy. Damn, I'll bet he looked surprised.

Том. I don't know anybody else who does it as much as Ben does.

Judy. It's not unbearably bad though, I suppose.

Том. I don't at all.

Willy. I don't either any more. I haven't in over a week.

Том. *He* sure did, but he won't now.

Judy. Dad said he can't remember a drier July in history.

Willy. Did you go down to the bridge?

Том. They're all finished. They hauled the last pile off this morning. I saw the truck go by.

Judy. A breeze would be nice.

Keith [*turning to her*]. I'm taking the muffler off the car tomorrow.

Judy. Clevis will jail you if you do; you know how he is.

Keith. I'll tell him it wore out and I'm getting a new one.

Judy. John tried that and he got a ticket anyway. Clevis said he shouldn't have drove it till he got the new one then.

Keith. They got somebody in jail.

Judy. When?

Keith. He may be out by now. He was probably just in overnight. We was talking to him last night. He's from Springfield. Lord, did he cuss out this town. Clevis would have put him up for a week if he could've heard him.

Judy. Why did they jail him in the first place?

Keith. Drunken driving. He said he wasn't, but you could tell he was.

Judy. How could you tell?

Keith. You could tell. We gave him a beer through the bars. He tried to give us a dollar for one can but we wouldn't take it.

Judy. You could be jailed yourself for talking to him.

Keith. There's no law. We shouldn't of had the beer, though. I just hope he doesn't slip and say something.

JUDY. He wouldn't.

KEITH. Well, he might, mad as he was. The Red Tavern in Nixa won't sell it any more. We had to go all the way to Rogersville to that place on the other side of town.

JUDY. It just looks like an awful lot of trouble for a headache to me.

KEITH. Tony was stopped last week—going around the square.

JUDY. Ummm.

KEITH. Clevis knew he was drunk as the Lord, but he didn't say anything. He's a nice guy, really, Clevis.

JUDY. Ummm.

KEITH. Billy Burt nearly knocked old Skelly down in the middle of Church Street yesterday. Old Skelly was standing in the road and swearing ninety-to-nothing, and Billy Burt just looked out and laughed.

JUDY. Ummm.

KEITH. He yelled back, "Why don't you watch where you're going, you old fool?" Clevis drove by and yelled to Skelly to shut up before he locked him up for disturbing the peace.

JUDY. What'd Skelly say to that?

KEITH. What'd you mean, what'd he say? Clevis told him to get the hell out of the middle of the street.

JUDY. I feel sorry for Skelly, someone like that. I really do.

TOM [very rapid, darting exchange; lightly]. Are you going to, too? Take it out.

WILLY. I'm not going to unless you do too.

TOM. Spit on it.

WILLY. What for?

TOM. It makes it slicker.

WILLY. I never heard of that.

TOM. Keep spitting on it; keep it wet. I'll race you.

The following two speeches are said simultaneously.

MARTHA [calling]. Carey? Car-ey?

WILLY. Okay, I'll race you.

MOTHER. Eat the crust too, Willy.

FATHER. Do what your mother tells you.

WILLY. I am.

MOTHER. No, you're not. I can see.

JUDY. Keith said he's gonna take the muffler off the car next Saturday. Either that or tomorrow.

MOTHER. Not tomorrow, I'd hope. That's nothing to do on a Sunday.

FATHER. Well, if he wants to pay a fine that's his business. You just better see he don't go blasting past here, waking me up.

MOTHER. Judy, don't say things to upset your father.

TED very distantly whistles to a dog.

JUDY. Billy Burt almost knocked Skelly down in the middle of Church Street.

WILLY. He drives like a maniac.

MOTHER. He'll get his license taken away from him if he isn't careful.

JUDY. Oh, he will not. Honestly, Clevis was right there and saw the whole thing. He just laughed. Skelly was cussing to beat the band. Clevis said he'd lock him up for disturbing the peace.

MOTHER. Are you gonna eat that crust?

WILLY. I don't like it, I tell you. I'll get sick. Honestly.

JUDY. Skelly ought to be locked up himself, anyway.

MOTHER. He hasn't hurt anybody. I feel sorry for him.

The following two speeches are said simultaneously.

TED [*distantly, calling*]. Blackie? Blackie? Here, Blackie.

FATHER. You do, do you?

MOTHER. Judy, I wish you wouldn't say things to upset your father.

The following two speeches are said simultaneously.

MARTHA [*calling*]. Carey? You come in here to dinner now.

WILLY. May I be excused please?

MOTHER. Willy, they're children in China starving for want of a crust of bread. They're children in China that will die this very night for the lack of that crust of bread.

WILLY. Well, send it to them then; don't make me eat it.

FATHER. You eat that, young man.

WILLY. It'll break my teeth. Feel how hard it is.

MOTHER. Your teeth aren't that tender.

MARTHA [*distantly singing, over a bit*].
>"Hush, little baby, don't say a word,
>Mama's gonna buy you a mockin' bird.
>If that mockin' bird don't sing,
>Mama's gonna buy you a diamond ring."

KEITH [*overlapping*]. Where you going so fast?

ALLISON. Home. Where would I be going?

KEITH. You always cut through the park?

ALLISON. I didn't see you, Keith Fellers, or I wouldn't have, smarty.

KEITH. Well, I saw you.

ELLIS. Do you feel any better now?

MANNY. I got to get home.

ELLIS. You feeling better?

TED. No. Worse if anything.

MANNY. I gotta get back home before long.

ELLIS. Drink another coffee maybe.

TED. No, I'll be sick again.

MANNY. You want to walk around the parking lot some more?

ELLIS. You need another black coffee.

TED. No. Come on. . . .

MANNY. Come on. Up you go.

ELLIS. You all right enough to go back in the café?

TED. I'll be okay.

ELLIS. You want a hamburger or something?

TED. Are you just trying to make me sick again? Don't talk about it.

MANNY. Some pie or something would settle your——

TED. —don't talk about it!

ELLIS. You didn't have any more to drink than the rest of us did.

TED. Well, I'm sorry.

MANNY. He didn't have as much. I don't even feel a buzz any more.

ELLIS. Look how white he is.

MANNY. Green.

ELLIS. I think he's passed out.

MANNY. I gotta get home.

ELLIS. We can't take him home like this.

MANNY. What are we going to tell his dad?

ELLIS. It's late already.

MANNY. I think he's passed out.

ELLIS. Teddy? Teddy?

TED. I'm okay. Stop shaking me around. Everything's spinning around.

MANNY. Are you going to be sick?

TED. I almost had the ground stopped moving around and you started shaking me around and started it all up again.

MANNY. He doesn't know what he's saying.

ELLIS. What are you going to tell your folks?

TED. I don't know, I told you.

MANNY. Well, look. We was out of gas way over past Nixa——

TED. No, no, no, I can't. . . .

MANNY. Why not? You got to say something.

TED. He'd never believe we ran out of gas. He'd never believe that one. Besides I've used that anyway.

MANNY. Well, a person can run out of gas more than once. It's a natural thing.

TED. He didn't believe it the other time.

ELLIS. Why not there was something in the gas line? And we thought we was out of gas and got it towed into Nixa?

TED [*feeling sick*]. Would you two quit talking about gas? Good God.

MANNY. Okay.

TED. What was we doing out past Nixa?

MANNY. Taking this girl home after the movie. Are you feeling better?

TED. A little.

MANNY. We better get back.

TED. I think I should try to eat something.

ELLIS. Oh, God.

MANNY. You said you didn't want anything.

TED. I think that would settle my stomach.

MANNY. Just a coke or something?

ELLIS. Are you feeling better? We gotta get home. You're looking better. You're standing a little better.

TED. Yeah, I'll be all right now.

MANNY. We'll get you another coffee.

TED. We won't say anything. I'll just sneak in.

ELLIS. Just so long as we get home before long.

MANNY. You'll be all right. Come on in.

ELLIS. We'll get you something to eat.

TED. Wait!

ELLIS. What's wrong?

TED. No, wait!

MANNY. Come on.

TED. I think I'm going to be sick again.

> ELLIS, MANNY, TED, PEGGY, and JUDY *all speak at once.*

ELLIS. Oh, my God, I knew it. Hell, we'll never get home.

MANNY. Jesus, watch out, then.

TED. Damn, I knew it. Oh, God.

PEGGY. That's lovely, it really is.

JUDY. And that's the living room.

JUDY [*continuing, dreamily but matter-of-factly; she and* PEGGY *are sitting on the porch steps*]. And the bedroom will be all in white. White walls, of course, and white ceiling. And white lace curtains with some floral pattern in them: white on white. And they'll be a dressing table with a white pleated skirt around it in silk. And a white silk bedspread and the rug will—uh, the floors in the bedroom will be just natural wood. And I'll grow African violets on the window sill in the bedroom because it'll get the south sun. And I'll have a white Scotty dog or white yarn cat like Mrs. Carters makes on the bed and a few white throw pillows, set up against the bed pillows there.

PEGGY. Mmmm. That's lovely. It really is. White on white.

JUDY. All in white. And then the kitchen will be green—a pale green, you know, and yellow—very sunny yellow. And they'll be cabinets in pale green and the floor and walls will be yellow and the

oven and stove and sink are all light green like the cabinets
and the ceiling is very small checks. Just green and yellow checks.
And the curtains—they'll be two windows, one over the sink and
one over the breakfast table—the curtains will be ruffled cotton.
Just plain polished cotton. And they're checks. And that's the
kitchen. And they'll be a stool to sit on. A high one. And that's
green with yellow and green checks on the top, upholstered. And
the counter—there's going to be a lot of counter space—and then
that's violet—no yellow. Like the floors. [*Pause.*] And the bedroom is violet and light brown. The walls are three of them violet
and the other one——

PEGGY [*remembering gently*]. You did the bedroom in white.

JUDY. Right. That's right. It's all in white. Everything in white.
With natural floors. But not a cold white. Not that white. A
kind of off-white.

PEGGY. Cream.

JUDY. No. More of an ivory.

PEGGY. Mmmm.

JUDY. And then the bathroom is all blue. Everything in blue.

WILLY [*calling lightly*]. Tommy? Tommy? If I whistle—listen—if I
whistle once, it means I'm coming up for sure. And if I whistle
two times, it means maybe, and three times, I don't know yet. You
got that? Once, I'm coming up, and two times, maybe, and three
times, I still don't know for sure—and four times means I'm not
coming up.

MAYBELLE. Is that lightning bugs over there, or is that someone in
your yard with a cigarette?

MOTHER. No, it's lightning bugs. See, they're in the back yard thick.

WILLY *whistles twice—twice—three times—three times—twice,
during the next line or two, keeping* TOMMY *posted.*

MAYBELLE. Can you see if Walt's going to bed or is he still in there
reading?

MOTHER. No, he's still reading the Bible.

MAYBELLE. He'll put his eyes out; he's not satisfied to be deaf. I'd
call in to him for all the good it'd do. He should be in bed. It's
past his bedtime. He's older than me eight years.

MOTHER. I know.

WILLY [*whistles one long note; beat*]. Tommy? Hey, Tommy?

MANNY [*sober, manly, brisk, as if moving around a pool table*]. Shit, that was a easyun, you just lucked that one in, a beginner woulda made thatun. That'll be the last for a while; shit, you just lucked out.

EARL [*nineteen, very manlyesque*]. Four in the side.

MANNY. Shit, you can't make that one. Better try the nine.

EARL. Shit I can't.

MANNY. Hell you can; I got six bits—two bits you can't.

EARL. Shit, that's an easyun.

MANNY. Shit it is; you better grease her up.

EARL. Watch this, shithead. [*Studies and shoots.*]

MANNY [*beat*]. Shit, you missed as good as a mile.

EARL. Hell I did. A little less English on thatun and it'd been just in there.

MANNY. Hell it would. Nine in the corner.

EARL. Four bits.

MANNY. Hell with you, too. You think I want to throw dough away? That's chicken feed.

EARL. Two bits.

MANNY. Hell, it's in there clean as a whistle. Watch this.

EARL [*quickly*]. Two bits?

MANNY. Hell yes. [*Studies and shoots.*]

EARL [*beat*]. We're even.

MANNY. Shit, that was almost in there.

EARL. Shit it was.

JUDY. Are you going to the movie tomorrow night?

PEGGY. When?

JUDY. Tomorrow night?

PEGGY. Oh, yeah. It's very good, actually. I saw it last year in Springfield. It's very good; I want to see it again. [*Beat.*] It's about this kinda island.

JUDY. During the war? I think I saw that one.

PEGGY. No, not that one. This one's in color.

JUDY. No, I didn't see that one then.

PEGGY. It's very good actually.

1ST FARMER [*a man of forty-five or so; overlapping just a word, ponderously slow*]. So I said to him. If you cut it green. And just let it lay. An extra day or two more. Then, you're gonna get—now, mind, you're not gonna get forty bales an acre—any fool'll tell you that. Not with your lespedeza. But your legume *hay*. Will go farther next *winter*. And they'll milk *more*. Than if you went for your forty bales to the acre and have it dry in the bale on you.

2ND FARMER [*also a farmer; he has grunted approval at least five times during the above*]. Providing it don't get wet in the field.

1ST FARMER. Oh, yeah.

2ND FARMER. That's the risk there.

1ST FARMER. Oh, yeah.

2ND FARMER. If it gets wet in the field, then it's ruined sure.

1ST FARMER. That's the way I put it to him. I told *him*. You cut it green. When it looks fair. And providing the weather looks like it's gonna hold. You just let it lay an extra day or two more.

MARTHA [*singing again, faintly, simultaneous with the* FARMER]:
"If that diamond ring turns brass,
    Mama's gonna buy you a lookin' glass."

MARTHA *continues to hum another verse.*

1ST FARMER [*continued from above*]. . . . And your lespedeza *hay*. Will be a sweeter *hay*. And they'll *milk more*. Than if you went for the forty bales an acre and have it dry in the bales on you.

The song continues a while after this.

KEITH [*overlapping the last of the song*]. You always cut through here, do you?

ALLISON. I do not. Don't you stand so close either.

KEITH. You been to prayer meeting or choir practice, I suppose?

ALLISON. If you went to church at all, you'd know that choir practice was on Tuesday early evenings and prayer meeting was on Wednesday nights.

KEITH. Do you want to go for a ride around?

ALLISON. No, thank you, I do not. I thought you was going steady with Judy Atkins recently.

KEITH. Well, I don't see her around right now, but you are.

ALLISON. I hope you don't think that makes me feel behoven to you. Just because she's not around just now.

KEITH. Besides, my hand might slip off the steering wheel and glance against your knee and you'd think you was being compromised or something.

ALLISON. I know what you're after and I'd think you should know better than to try something like that with me. You may have a car and all, but that doesn't matter a hill of beans as far as I'm concerned.

KEITH. Are you too holy for a little making out, are you?

ALLISON. I happen to know Judy Atkins very well, and you better let me on by.

KEITH. Does she talk about me to you?

ALLISON. I would say she does, yes, she sometimes does. But don't ask me what because I'm not saying.

KEITH. But I'll bet it just makes you squirm, doesn't it?

ALLISON. No. It certainly does not. Make me squirm. What do you mean, it just makes me squirm? Let me on by.

KEITH. You don't have to get so hot under the collar.

ALLISON. I'm not getting hot under the collar or anywhere el— you just let me go on home now.

KEITH. Why?

MOTHER [calling]. Willy?

ALLISON. Come on.

KEITH. Why?

MOTHER [calling]. Willy?

ALLISON. Come on.

KEITH. Why, she won't have to know. [He puts an arm around her neck.]

ALLISON. [pulling away, but rather reluctantly]. That has nothing to do with it. Just keep your hands where they belong too.

KEITH. You're more amply built.

ALLISON. Judy is just thin—you keep your hands away.

KEITH. You want to drive up to Harper's Hill?

ALLISON. What would Judy think of that?

KEITH. She wouldn't know.

ALLISON. I suppose she goes up there with you.

KEITH. Did she tell you that?

ALLISON. I didn't say she told me everything. Besides everyone would see us going through town and on the highway.

KEITH. You'd like to, though, wouldn't you?

ALLISON. No, I would not.

KEITH. Sure you would.

ALLISON. I have to go home.

KEITH. I could drive you home after the hill.

ALLISON. No, thank you.

KEITH. I've seen you watching me.

ALLISON. I have not. I suppose you think if you're the basketball hero of the town and all, every girl is ready to just jump right into your lap; well, you've got another think coming.

KEITH. I know you have. I've seen you.

ALLISON. I haven't, I told you. I've seen you looking at me enough, and at every other girl around.

KEITH. Well, if you noticed that, you must have been looking.

ALLISON. Come on, I didn't say that.

KEITH. You want to sit in the car awhile?

ALLISON. No. I might sit here in the park, but not in your car.

KEITH. This is fine with me. Clevis might come by, though.

ALLISON. Nobody ever comes by here. I come through here every night and I've not seen anybody.

KEITH. I knew you would.

ALLISON [*a bit more confused, intense*]. I have noticed you; I couldn't help noticing you. That doesn't mean anything.

KEITH. I knew you wanted to.

ALLISON. I didn't say I wanted to do anything except just sit and talk.

KEITH. All right we'll just sit and talk.

Everyone else is standing, looking off in different directions. They begin moving around, beginning slowly, becoming more urgent, faster and louder.

ALLISON. That's all.

MOTHER. Willy?

KEITH. . . . Not all. . . .

The lines flow one immediately after the other, building.

PEGGY. . . . Fine. . . .

MANNY. . . . In the corner. . . .

ALLISON. . . . Yes. . . .

EARL. . . . Four in the side. . . .

KEITH. . . . Okay? . . .

ALLISON. . . . No. . . .

JUDY. . . . No. . . .

MOTHER. . . . Willy! . . .

WILLY. . . . What? . . .

JUDY. . . . Isn't it . . .

MOTHER. . . . Will-y! . . .

WILLY. . . . What? . . .

JUDY. . . . just . . .

WILLY. . . . What do you want! . . .

JUDY. . . . lovely?! . . .

MOTHER. . . . Come on, now. . . .

KEITH. . . . Okay? . . .

PEGGY. . . . Yes! . . .

ALLISON. . . . Yes! . . .

PEGGY. . . . Yes, it is! . . .

FATHER [*very loud*]. . . . *Willy!* . . .

WILLY. . . . All right! . . .

MARTHA [*loud, sustained call lasting through* KEITH'S "Take it easy!"]. Car—e-y!

The following short speeches are rapid, loud, urgent.

ALLISON. Keith!

MANNY. Hell you can!

KEITH. Take it easy!

ALLISON. *I love you so!*

MARTHA [*singing, beginning with* ALLISON's *last word and continuing through the next few speeches*].

> "Hush little baby, don't say a word,
> Mama's gonna buy you a mockin' bird.
> If that mockin' bird don't sing,
> Mama's gonna buy you a diamond ring.
> If that diamond ring turns brass,
> Mama's gonna buy you a lookin' glass.
> If that lookin' glass gets broke——"

WILLY [*very softly, slowly rising in intensity*]. Tommy? Tommy? Listen. If I whistle once it means I'm coming up for sure, and if I whistle two times it means maybe and three times, I don't know yet. You got that? . . . [*Fades at end.*]

KEITH [*cued by* WILLY's *"whistle," very softly, slowly rising in intensity*]. Billy Burt nearly knocked old Skelly down in the middle of Church Street yesterday. Old Skelly was standing in the road and swearing ninety-to-nothing and Billy Burt just looked out and laughed. . . . [*Fades away near the end.*]

1ST FARMER [*cued by* KEITH's *"Old," begins not too soft, fades near the end*]. So I said to him. If you cut it green. And just let it lay. An extra day or two more. Now you're gonna get. Now mind, you're not gonna get forty bales to the acre. Not with your lespedeza. . . .

MOTHER [*cued by "said"*]. Willy, there are children in China starving for the want of that crust of bread. They're children in China that will die this very night. . . .

KEITH's *line should extend past the others a word or so, as the song ends.*

JUDY [*immediately after the song, overlapping* KEITH's *line just a bit*]. And the bedroom's all in various shades of violet. With violets printed on all the sheets.

WILLY [*answering back, as though from his bedroom, softly*]. You think Keith will like that?

JUDY. Oh, I'm sure. Violet's practically his favorite color.

MOTHER [*softly calling*]. You kids get to bed in there now. Judy. Willy, I don't want to hear another peep out of you two.

JUDY. I am.

ALLISON. We shouldn't've done that! Oh, God, I think I got my dress all—— [*She stops before going up on the porch.*]

Everyone circling.

ELLIS. You feeling better now? Hey, Teddy, you feeling better?

MANNY. What the hell are you gonna tell your dad?

TED. I guess that we ran out of gas on the other side of Nixa if he's awake.

ELLIS. You feeling all right?

TED. I'm okay, don't worry about me. I'll be all right.

MAYBELLE [*On the porch; loudly, as though talking to someone deaf*]. *Walt? Are you going to stay up reading all night?*

JUDY [*calling softly*]. Willy? Are you sleepy? Are you asleep?

MAYBELLE. *I said are you going to come to bed now?*

WILLY [*sleepy, softly calling to Judy, as though from his room*]. No.

WALT [*loudly, as though talking to someone deaf; he is very old*]. *I heard you. I'll be along.*

JUDY. Have you decided what you're gonna be? Are you gonna be an artist like you said?

MAYBELLE. *You're gonna read and ruin your eyes.*

MOTHER. [*begins to hum "All My Trials" very softly—a lullaby*].

WILLY. I don't know. I been thinking I might be a writer like for the newspapers.

WALT. *I heard you. I'm all right.*

JUDY. I just want to be a good mother. A good wife and a good mother. You know?

WILLY. Uh-huh.

MAYBELLE. *What are you a-doing tomorrow?*

JUDY. How come you aren't going to be an artist? When did you decide?

WALT. *I'll probably go up to the post office if it's clear.*

WILLY. I thought I might be an artist on the side kinda. And if I write pieces for the paper too, then I could write pieces about *Nature*. And make people *really notice* Nature. You know?

JUDY. That'd be nice . . . that'd be a very good thing to do.

MAYBELLE. *Are you gonna hear the alarm?*

WILLY. One piece I thought I'd write would be all about here. Only it'd be about the Nature around us all the time and that we never notice. You know?

JUDY. Uh-huh.

MAYBELLE. *There ain't no mail tomorrow, it's a Sunday.*

WILLY. It would be just about the *wonders* of Nature. And I'd have a lot of characters and they'd all talk; only they'd all be things in Nature around us all the time. Like it would be a countryside. And the tree would talk and tell all about itself; like about its getting a new ring every year, you know?

JUDY. Uh-huh.

MAYBELLE [*to herself*]. There ain't no mail tomorrow, it's a Sunday.

WILLY. And the meadow would talk. And the brook would talk like a laugh kinda. And the hills would talk and the berry bushes like about the food they supply to wild animals and the wheat fields and things.

MAYBELLE. *There's nothing doing on a Sunday.* You ought not to walk up that hill in this heat.

JUDY. That's beautiful.

WILLY. Just about all of Nature and all.

JUDY. That's really lovely. It is. Wild animals.

WILLY. And they'd tell all about themselves.

MAYBELLE. *You hear?*

JUDY. I sure do want to see it when you do it.

WALT. *I'll just go up a bit and see what's doing.*

No one moves except JUDY *and* WILLY.

WILLY. And I figure they'd each one have a little speech that they'd just say out directly about themselves like: "This is the rill speaking over here. They've been tearing down that old bridge down by the fork there. . . ."

JUDY. What's a rill?

WILLY. You know, like "I love thy rocks and rills."

JUDY. Oh, sure. That's nice. Are you sleepy now?

WILLY. Yes. Are you going to the movie tomorrow? Judy? Good night.

JUDY. Good night, Willy.

The others stir gently now, walk gently around.

WILLY. Good night, Judy.

JUDY. Good night, Mother.

MOTHER. Good night.

WILLY. Good night, Mother.

MOTHER. You two go on to bed in there now.

MAYBELLE. You come on in. [*She steps off the porch and stands motionless.*]

KEITH *whistles for his dog, softly, distantly. He takes a few steps and stands motionless. The lights are quite dim.*

JUDY *and* WILLY. Good night, Daddy.

FATHER. That's enough now. [*He stands motionless.*]

JUDY. Well, good night.

FATHER [*after a brief pause*]. Good night.

Everyone is standing, quite still. The MOTHER *continues to hum a few soft notes of the song. The light on the porch fades.*